RETURN
TO
HEAVEN

TIM McCABE

McCabe, Tim.
        Return to heaven : a world war II pilot's life, death and journey
beyond… / Tim McCabe.

ISBN 9781686360480
Independently published by the Author

Book Design & Cover Image © Tim McCabe
Background photo: Shutterstock

Visit us online at **www.returntoheavenbook.com**

Follow *Return to Heaven* on Facebook and Instagram

To Dad

"I have spoken to you of earthly things
and you do not believe; how then will you
believe if I speak of heavenly things?"

JOHN 3:12

— CONTENTS —

The following is a letter from Jim, to his son, Jimmy….

— 1 —
The LAST SHOT

Dear Jimmy,

It was a hot one out. On August 19, 1993, the weatherman said it was supposed to get up to ninety-six degrees. However, as the day wore on, the humidity of the muggy St. Louis summer pushed the index well over one hundred. There was no wind on the golf course that day, and the air seemed swollen from the thick heat.

We were playing up in St. Charles which was our usual spot. I was seventy years old, and I was out doing what I did on most Thursday mornings in those days—playing eighteen holes with Tom, Wally and Bob.

Before we had headed out for our round, I happened to tell Tom that I wasn't feeling like myself. In fact, I had said the exact thing to your mother that morning when I was getting ready.

She suggested that I consider taking it easy instead of going with the guys. So, yes, I thought about it, but of course I went out and played anyway.

On that particular day, all my drives were landing in the fairway... so, I guess I should have known that something wasn't right. In the back of my mind, I knew I was down to less than a quarter of a functioning heart after the previous two heart attacks had inflicted so much damage. Almost twelve years had passed since the quadruple bypass, and I suppose I was officially on borrowed time.

It was my turn to hit, so I walked up to the tee box and bent down to put the ball on the tee. Then, when I stood up, the whole scene in front of me spun as I felt a drop in my chest. My head was reeling; I guess the best way to describe it was that in pilot's terms, I was losing pressure in the cabin.

I steadied myself on my driver. Wally yelled something at me but I waved him off. I approached the ball and glanced back at the fellas, who were really paying attention now.

I lined up my shot and let it rip—and believe it or not, it went straight.

I watched that ball sail right down the middle of the fairway, bounce and land just like it's supposed to do. It laid up quite nicely.

"Dammit," I thought to myself.

I could feel my heart failing. This time, there was no sensation like some giant rubber band squeezing me hard around the ribs. There was no elephant jumping up and down on my sternum, causing me to double over in pain. Not anymore—the little muscle that had caused me so much panic over the years had nothing left. The emergency system was gone; drained of all its power.

Time slowed to a trickle. This was it. Strangely, I could feel the warm sun on the back of my neck, and I heard the chirping of birds. I remember thinking to myself, that, all things considered, it was not such a bad way to go.

Walking off the tee box, I somehow made it back to the cart and sat down next to Wally, who looked at me with an expression of shock and demanded we head back to the clubhouse. Tom, my good friend for so many years, ran over and grabbed my arm.

"Come on, Jim," I heard him say. "Let's get you back."

And then, I slumped over dead in the golf cart....

— 2 —
"*An* INHERENT APTITUDE *for* FLYING"

Jimmy, I need to tell you about my time in the war. By now, I'm sure you've probably gone through all of my old belongings... the tin boxes, the faded photos, the yellowed files. I suppose I left behind enough items that you can piece most everything together from my life. But I want to tell you what I *really* experienced. I want to tell you *my* story, Jimmy. And, someday, I hope that you will tell me yours.

I was eighteen years old in 1941, and I was just six months out of high school with no idea what I was going to do next with my life. In fact, I was hanging out at a place called Carpenter's Soda Shop playing a pinball machine when I heard the cut-in on the radio, reporting that the Japanese had just attacked Pearl Harbor.

I was still living with my parents. Years earlier in 1929, they had lost their savings when the stock market crashed. They had salvaged enough money to send my two older brothers to college; but, by 1941, there wasn't enough left for me to follow.

That radio announcement changed so many families' worlds, and ours was no different. My older brothers, your Uncle Don and Uncle Bill, enlisted right away. Bill loved to write poetry and was good at mechanics—he became a radio operator in the Army and was stationed in North Africa.

My oldest brother, Don, was a fantastic artist and very meticulous. He applied for flight school to train as a pilot, and was cleared to fly bombers. The oldest of the four of us kids, Don's calm temperament made him a perfect fit for a bomber crew. After Don made it through flight school, I knew exactly what I wanted to do when I enlisted, too.

Knowing that Don had earned his wings made me think that I might also have a chance. I figured that it beat being mired in the mud somewhere halfway across the world in the infantry. Not that I really wanted to be up in one of those big bombers, though... they were awkward to fly and slow to react. The B-24 Liberators that Don would be flying were nicknamed "Flying Coffins," and I decided that if I ever made it through flight school, I would need to be flying something a lot faster and nimbler than a coffin.

My goal was to become a fighter pilot.

———

My parents had just sent two of their three sons off to the war. Since I was the youngest, my mother asked me to wait until at least my nineteenth birthday before I enlisted. When March 3, 1942 finally arrived, I packed up my things, said goodbye to my mom and dad, and left... leaving only my older sister Nancy behind.

Army basic training began April, 1942, and a few months later I was accepted into Flight Training School as an Aviation Cadet. I started flying in Pine Bluff, Arkansas, and then graduated to the Gulf Coast Army Air Forces Training Center at Randolph Field in Texas.

"The duties of an Army Pilot call for a high degree of mental and physical alertness, sound judgement and an inherent aptitude for flying," the Major General bragged in a letter to my parents. "In order to win this war, it is vital to have the best-qualified young men at the controls of our military aircraft."

But those were just platitudes for the parents; we really didn't know what we were doing up there. The statistics show that U.S. air training in the Second World War was just as dangerous as the actual combat. We were all eighteen and nineteen years old, and we were green. The only way for cadets to gain experience was to get up there and start flying, and we logged a lot of flight hours and in all kinds of weather.

Cadets started in small trainer planes, like the PT-19 two-seaters, where the instructors would sit behind us on our beginning flights. I made my first solo flight June 27, 1942 in one of those trainers. Eventually, we worked up to the larger planes like the BT-14, a big 450-horsepower bird, and we would take those up all by ourselves to better build our confidence.

If we weren't flying, we were out doing mechanical work on the aircraft in the field. And if we weren't doing that, we were learning in the classroom with an instructor showing us maneuvers using small model planes. The commanders taught us the differences between the aircrafts, the basics of aerodynamics, and how to maintain our angles of attack. After we had mastered the fundamentals, they taught us how to approach a target, engage in air-to-air combat, and practice gunnery. The wash-out rate for cadets was high. Instructors inundated us with information to make sure we learned how to process a barrage of data quickly... and do it correctly.

Those were the days of leather helmets and plastic goggles, and there wasn't much between a pilot and the sky around him except for a thin bubble of glass over his head.

We had our radio and instruments in front of us, but when we lost visibility up in the clouds we just had to figure it out. So much of learning was just flying by the seat of our pants, Jimmy.

Guys could panic when they lost their bearings in the sky. Then, they would head straight back down as soon as they caught a glimmer of light through a clearing in the clouds below. In fact, that's exactly what happened after I had completed just a few months of training from the aviation grounds at Randolph Field.

On the morning of September 17, 1942, I was in a single prop plane idling on the runway, waiting to take off. The cloud ceiling was very low that day and fog was covering the airfield. Because of the weather conditions, flight control was struggling to keep track of all the planes coming in and going out.

The flight deck radioed in and gave me the "all clear" for takeoff. My lights were on as I throttled the engine and accelerated down the strip. I lifted off and took my time pushing up into the headwind.

Suddenly, coming out of the clouds, I saw the lights of another plane dropping straight towards me. I was only a few meters off the ground and there was nowhere for me to go to avoid a collision.

The other plane nosedived beneath me. As it skidded towards the landing strip underneath my plane, my back wheel crashed through the other aircraft's cockpit, killing the pilot instantly. My plane lurched forward and slammed hard into the ground—the collision was a blur of noise and pain. Inside my cockpit, I saw blood on the dash and I grabbed my face... my nose and cheeks felt like soft mush... and that's the last thing I remember before losing consciousness.

———

I was pulled from the wreckage and rushed to the field hospital where the medical staff stabilized me. Despite the violence of the crash, I had somehow managed to escape with only a broken nose and a swollen face. However, I had residual problems with my vision which stunted my training; it would take several months for me to fully recover from the reconstructive surgeries on my face.

The Army never told me much about the details of what happened that day. No one gave me a report on the other pilot; no one explained what had gone wrong on the flight deck. What I do know is that over 15,000 American pilots died in training alone, never making it to the real war.

Crashes happened fairly frequently, and in wartime, everyone just had to keep pushing forward.

As I lay there in the hospital bed, slowly regaining clarity, I knew that if I ever wanted to earn my wings and continue flying I had to get back up in the air. Eventually, my faculties returned and I finished my medical treatment. I was cleared to get back in the cockpit where I logged the rest of my hours without incident and earned my wings. I had survived training, and was referred to Advanced Flying School.

————

Our present day Air Force did not exist back then, so it was the Army that put me in a Republic P-47 Thunderbolt heavy fighter and sent me off to England in October, 1943. I was stationed with the 19th Tactical Air Command, imbedded with the Eighth Air Force in the European Theater. We were the 367th Fighter Bomber Squadron, or, as we called ourselves, The Thunderbirds.

Our insignia was an embroidered vulture, flying in a storm cloud, grasping in its clutches a pair of lightning bolts. It was fitting, as the Thunderbird pilots of the 367th were bold, and many guys were in it for the adrenaline rush. We had heard all the stories about the German Aces in the Luftwaffe, with their superior air power. From the day we graduated Advanced Training School and became fighters, we wanted to prove that *we* were the best.

The P-47 Thunderbolt was a relatively new kind of attack fighter that gave us the confidence we needed in the sky. She was a prop fighter that was versatile, and the Thunderbolt suited me just fine. It was a dive bomber, a fighter escort, a sweeper, and a reconnaissance plane all in one. With the Thunderbolts, we could carry bombs for sorties or we could head up with nothing but our eight 50-caliber guns for high altitude air-to-air attacks. No pilot had a specific plane assigned to him because the field mechanics were constantly working on the fleet. We would fly whichever plane was ready to go on the day of our mission.

Yet, on the base in England, pilots were allowed to name a plane in the group. One of the guys in the squadron had a knack for illustration, and he would paint whatever we wanted on the nose after it had been approved by the command.

I knew that a leggy lady painted on my plane would have been bad luck for me... not necessarily in the skies, but certainly if I ever made it back to go on a date with your mom again. There was a popular cartoon woodpecker back in those days that used to fly around and hammer his beak on everything. That bird was fast and looked like he did a lot of damage, so I asked the base artist to paint a similar character on the front of my plane. I named that plane the *Lil' Pecker*.

Looking back at all my combat missions against the Germans, neither the *Lil' Pecker* nor the other planes I flew ever let me down in the sky. I don't know if it was the training back in Texas or the P-47's powerful Double Wasp engine that kept me safest, but the Thunderbolt fit me like a glove and I took to her quite naturally.

I started flying combat missions in November, 1943. We started out mostly running patrols over the English Channel, a body of water with which I would soon become very familiar. By December, we were sweeping the French beaches, and, by January 1944, our squadron was dive bombing Nazi forces throughout the European mainland.

All throughout 1944, we made raids deep into Germany alongside the British Air Force. We definitely got our chance to prove ourselves against those pilots of the Third Reich. Sometimes, we would be sent on as many as three runs in a day. From February 20 through February 25, 1944, our squadron engaged in the attacks of Operation Argument, also known as "The Big Week."

During the Big Week, we hit the German air forces right in the heart of their country—attacking air strips, hangars, communication hubs and factories. The skies near any Reich airfield were always a mess, and those same skies would fill with anti-aircraft fire and enemy planes the closer we got to our targets. While we inflicted massive damage on the Nazi air forces during that operation, it came at a terrible price. We lost a total of over 250 bomber and fighter aircraft during the operation. Over 2,000 US airmen were either captured or killed during that week alone.

Back on our own base, we debriefed and reported all that had happened to Allied planes that did not return. Yes, we often observed planes being shot down from all around us. Sometimes they splashed into the Atlantic Ocean, and sometimes they spun into the grounds of Europe... forever laid to rest wherever they landed far below.

We described the loss of one of our fellow pilots as having had his plane "auger in." Seeing a plane corkscrew down in a trail of smoke was terrifying, and it happened too frequently, Jimmy. Statistics show that the total casualties of airmen lost over Europe was higher than Marines lost in the Pacific. But we didn't know the stats back then. We only knew that we had lost our friends... and any time we went up, we knew that we could be next.

———

Our squadron had to stay focused on the missions at hand. We were nicknamed "The Work Horse Group," because of how many combat missions we had already flown by the spring of 1944.

Although we were all fighter pilots, we weren't what you would call glamour boys. Many of us were from the Midwest. Like me, Fred Hillis, Robert Oberschelp, Francis Schilly, Lester Ross and Darrel Boyer were from Missouri. There was Gene Woodyard from Ohio, Cermel Shook from North Carolina, Jimmy Tipton from Arkansas, and Louis Wilson from West Virginia. We all trusted each other and had a pretty good idea of what to expect when we went up as a team. We became friends on the ground because we were brothers in the air.

We engaged the Nazis over German territory the entire month of March, 1944. Our missions ranged from squadron escort duty, to tactical bombing, and everything in between. The pilots who were next to me displayed the courage and skill needed for success. Many in our squadron were awarded decorations for "meritorious achievement while participating in missions over enemy territory," according to Brigadier General Quesada, Commanding General of the 9th Fighter Command. A lot of Air Medals and Bronze Oak Leaf Clusters were earned by our pilots during the springtime missions of '44.

———

In April, our 19th Tactical Air Command attacked ground targets across France from up high and down low, dive bombing airports and factories. We swooped in over the treetops and attacked the occupying forces entrenched in the French countryside. German machine gunners would sit in the upper stories of the stone farmhouses and empty their rounds at us headlong from the windows. Sometimes, we would make a descent into a rural village to take out a railroad depot or similar target. Green hedgerows would suddenly flash as strands of tracer fire roped towards us. We knew from our recon missions that France was absolutely crawling with Nazis: from the beaches to the cities.

Meanwhile, Patton's Army was making the push on the ground. The General himself had requested our "Work Horses" to provide cover for his soldiers as they moved through Europe. That was something the guys and I took great pride in, Jimmy.

On June 5, 1944, our group was flying over Paris, hitting railroads as we had often done before. Operation Overlord started at nightfall, and the invading D-Day forces convoyed over the Channel on June 6, hitting the beaches that morning. It was our squadron's job to continue the attacks on enemy reinforcements behind the battle lines, deep into France. When the boys on the ground broke through at Normandy, the 367th hammered the Nazis back through Germany all summer long.

———

When we escorted the bombers into Germany, our main targets were enemy complexes and supply zones miles below us. Our small planes couldn't carry the fuel that the big bombers could. However, on short and mid-range flights, we could occasionally make it all the way to the bullseye along with the rest of the squadron.

There was only one way to get our heavy payloads over those fortified German cities, Jimmy. We had to stay high and tight with the big boys until we were all within sight of the target. Then, our fighter group would dive down hard and all hell would break loose. The German anti-aircraft rounds would come in at us from the ground, allowing the bombers to unload their bays from up above. The Germans might have been known for their blitzkriegs, but we called this a "ramrod."

Now your Uncle Don was piloting one of those big birds somewhere over the Atlantic. We had hung out back in London once or twice, stealing a couple nights out at the bars when we could. But now we were stationed on separate bases, and that's about all I knew of my brother's whereabouts.

It was around the middle of June now, and it seemed like the entire Eighth Air Force was running back and forth over the North Sea, bombing Hamburg and other industrial cities. My group was assigned to escort a squadron of Liberators carrying all sorts of ordnance for a raid into Hannover. We had a rough flight into northern Germany, bringing us right into the belly of the beast, and I remember guys getting hit and planes spinning down all over the place.

I'm telling you, Jimmy, in my Thunderbolt I had real freedom. Even when the enemy was all over us, I could still maneuver. I would glance over at those poor fellas in the bombers and they looked like sitting ducks. We fighters did everything we could to keep them protected, for as long as we could stay with them.

That day over Hannover, I told the Liberator crew right next to me the same thing that I'm telling you, Jimmy. I told them that our fighter group was there to cover them.

I remember the flak, and I remember the crackling voice that came back over the radio telling me that they appreciated everything we fighters did for them.

I don't know how our group got out of there in one piece that day, Jimmy, but we did. When I got back on the ground, one of the radio guys came up and asked me if I knew who the pilot of the bomber was that I was escorting on that mission. I said I did not. He told me that the flight command figured out I had been flying next to my own brother, B-24 Liberator pilot Don McCabe. I asked where Don was, and they shunted me over to see him at a separate base. I jumped off the jeep and sure enough... what a surprise to see him, Jimmy.

We hung out for the day, and the crew let me pilot his bomber on a little fun run. That's just a testament to the mood of the base when Don and I showed up together, reunited. Nobody flew anything on base without authorization, but I took off in that Liberator and then landed it on a dime in front of Don's whole crew. I think it really tickled him. And let me tell you, compared to a fighter, landing one of those bombers took the strength of two men and a boy just to control the wings.

During the bombing mission over Hannover, I earned the Distinguished Flying Cross award, and Don earned another Air Medal for helping bring all his boys home safely. Don was a calm and conscientious pilot, and his crew loved him just like I did. A press release from the War Department reported our unique experience on that mission, and it was picked up by all the local papers.

I wondered what my mom and dad must have thought when they were notified, then later saw the headline in the morning news: "Brothers Fight in Same Raid Over Reich Without Knowing It." The Star-Times stated, "Two St. Louis brothers recently were reunited in the air over Germany, but they didn't realize it until later when they met - on the ground - in England. The brothers are 1st Lt. James J. McCabe, a Thunderbolt pilot, and 2nd Lt. Harry Don McCabe, Jr., a Liberator pilot, sons of Mr. and Mrs. Harry D. McCabe, Sr."

Imagine my parents' surprise when they read that I had unknowingly escorted my big brother and his crew on a bombing run through Germany.

———

In July, our Thunderbird group was one of the first to move over to a new air base in France. The Army was still setting up the airfield when we arrived, and Germans launched rockets on the grounds while we were bringing in the equipment and aircraft.

By August 1944, the Supreme Headquarters of the Allied Command had followed us over the English Channel, moving their headquarters from England to France. The front had moved, and Allied leadership followed.

Yet, the orders coming down from above didn't change our regular missions much. On our days off, we still listened to British radio stations or caught some rays on the lawn outside our tents. We exercised and had meals in the barracks, and we had it much better than those infantry boys stuck out on the frontlines.

One day, my fellow pilot, Cermel Shook, was flying back to base after having his plane shot full of holes. Just a few miles from our airfield, he spotted a lone German soldier speeding away on a motorcycle down below. The cyclist looked up and saw a sputtering American Thunderbolt bearing down on him, and the frightened cyclist sped up and flipped right off the road.

Shook made it to base and then went out and recovered that Jerry motorcycle. After that, whenever Cermel had a day off, he would take us joyriding around the French countryside on his new bike.

———

By late summer, we had already dropped thousands of tons of bombs on the Germans; our group alone would often make over twenty runs in a day. We were patrolling enemy skies, and it was common for pilots to return to base with their planes smoking and full of holes.

Quite often, we had no flight details until right before takeoff. This could especially happen when flying an escort mission—we might take off and be ordered back after we were already halfway across France. Once airborne, missions could be changed or aborted completely. We didn't know what to expect up there, other than that it would be very cold in the cockpit.

Our legs and toes would be freezing cold, but our faces and necks would be sweating from the sun beating in through the glass. There was no bathroom, and, on a long run, we had to stay in formation while we wrestled our layers off to urinate on the floor. Back on the ground, you wanted to get out of that seat as soon as you landed.

On September 2, 1944, I was sent up to escort a plane carrying one of the generals. When we arrived at the Allied base, I saw General Dwight Eisenhower get off that same plane we had been covering. He met with several of the field officers, and, just a few hours later, we escorted him safely back to Headquarters. That was quite a return flight, when the boys and I realized exactly who we were protecting in the air.

By October, I had so many missions scratched on the side of the *Lil' Pecker* that I was one of the vets. They gave me a thirty day leave of absence because of the many missions I had logged, and you can bet I took it... even though my tour was technically almost up.

I went back home to my mother and father on Julian Avenue, and then I made a beeline to see your mom. I put on my best uniform, and I asked her to marry me... and I tell you, Jimmy, *that* made me nervous. She said yes, and your mom and I got married while I was on leave, November 18, 1944.

Finally, in 1945, after a year and a half of training and 98 completed combat missions in the European Theater of

World War II, my service as an officer and pilot in the United States Army was over.

Or so I thought.

— 3 —
MY ENCOUNTER *with the* LORD

Maybe I could have lived to be a hundred if I hadn't have had such a bad heart, Jimmy. When your mom and I first met, she called me a "hood" and didn't like that I had been smoking cigarettes since I was eleven. It turns out she was right—they were really bad for me.

My first attack at the age of fifty-three was a big one, and it damaged a lot of the tissue in my heart. It happened at the handball club, and I had to be taken to the hospital by two guys in the clubhouse. My good friend, John Gilmore, later told me that I came close to breaking his hand, I was grasping it so hard in the car. When we finally arrived at the emergency room, I collapsed and they punched a needle in my heart. That type of heart attack is known as a widow maker, and how I made it through, I still don't know.

But, as you are aware, Jimmy, it was the second heart attack that almost ended it for me. I was fifty-nine, and by then there was so much arterial damage that they had to put me under the knife for a quadruple bypass. Keep in mind that in 1982, a surgery like that was a big deal.

24

Do you remember visiting me in the ICU after that operation, Jimmy? Your mom was there with me the whole time. She said that I was asleep and recuperating when the nurses brought you in to my room. The operation had gone well, all things considered, and they had just taken me over to my new recovery ward. At least the hardest part seemed to be over.

As soon as you and the rest of the family had gathered around me, I flatlined. The machines went off and there was a commotion; the nurses all rushed in and they made you leave.

The reason I know this is that suddenly, I was totally aware of everything. Did you know that I could see you, Jimmy? I watched the nurses ask you to leave. You, your siblings and your mother all looked back at me. I saw the staff scramble around, the doctor rush in, and then I saw them hit me with the paddles.

My view was from up near the ceiling and it was all so strange. Peaceful, really. In fact, I remember wishing they would be a little gentler on that old fella in the bed.

I saw the body in bed jump, but I couldn't feel it. There was no cardiac arrest happening where I was. Imagine realizing that you are both conscious *and* outside your body. So, this is what it felt like to check out, I thought.

St. Paul, himself, had something similar happen to him when he wrote, "Whether it was in the body or out of the body I do not know—God knows" (2 Cor 12:3). I can tell you, Jimmy, God knows I was most definitely outside of my body.

As soon as I became aware of where I was, I started moving backward, up through the ceiling, and out above the hospital. I saw the roof, the helicopter pad, and the parking lot below. I rose above the highway as the trees all started to shrink away. And then slowly, gracefully, I rotated towards the sky.

———

Several years later I was talking to your sister, Peggy. I just couldn't figure out why I was sent back. I suppose I really wasn't "sent back" as much as given a choice. The Lord's voice was so tender, but so authoritative. It was a Father's voice, but not the same voice as my own dad's from years before on Earth. This was the voice of the Father in Heaven.

I knew He wanted me to return. His voice is like the rushing of many waters, just as the Bible tells us, Jimmy. He asked me, "Jim, my son. Do you want to go back, or come home?"

That was it. What would you say? I had seen a thousand sunsets in the skies above, but I had never seen a Light like that. I wanted to go towards that beautiful Light more than anything in the world. This was The Creator and He was inviting me home. On Earth I was tired, I was in pain, and I knew that if I went back, I would be facing a difficult recovery... again.

God spoke directly into my heart—that old, hurting heart of mine. He spoke right into it and His voice was so familiar, Jimmy. I knew I could go with Him to Heaven if I just asked, yet I also knew He was nudging me back to Earth...

———

...BOOM... BOOM... BOOM...

Huge pillars fell around me. They were tall and white as snow. They glowed with power and the columns came down in a row. The corridor to His Eternal Kingdom was forming like a great hall in front of me. With each beat of my heart, they dropped and I could feel myself being slowly loosened from my earthly body. It seemed to all happen in an instant, or maybe an eternity, yet time was running out. I knew that if the last column dropped, I would be separated from the physical world forever.

The Bible tells of the great decorated columns called Boaz and Jachin—the holy boundaries of Solomon's Temple (1 Kings 7:21-22). A row of pillars guards the inner sanctum of God's Holy of Holies, and in order to enter His dwelling, one must be made anew. Now the wall separating me from God's Kingdom was right in front of me: the barrier between this world and the next.

But I wasn't going. I felt heavy and I just couldn't let go. The Lord waited for my answer, and I told Him I wanted to go back. Immediately my chest throbbed, I fell back through the room, the beeping returned, and I was revived.

———

There is no playbook on how to recover from yet another heart attack. When I awoke, I was confused. So many thoughts filled my head as I felt the tubes in my throat. I had struggled with a bad heart, and I feared the pain that came when I was resuscitated. I wrestled with the fact that I had just glimpsed eternity… and now it was gone.

I was really depressed, in case you and the rest of the family hadn't noticed.

One day, months later, as my emotional condition worsened, your mother sat down next to me and we had a discussion. I believe her exact words were, "You need to snap out of it."

You might think I had been encouraged by my experience... spiritually and physically regenerated. On one hand, I had seen the gates of Heaven; on the other hand, I just wanted to get healthy enough to play a round of golf again.

Eventually I got better, and I got stronger.

I finally told your mom what had happened to me that day in the ICU, and to my surprise, she believed me. Eventually, I came to accept that my time had not yet come. To my surprise, the Lord gave me nearly twelve more years with my family on Earth.

———

Now here I found myself, those twelve years later, on the golf course and once again outside my body. This time, I wasn't hovering in some hospital room, but just off the tee box. It really didn't surprise me after having gone through this all once before.

What did surprise me was seeing how fast the fellas ran towards me when they saw me slouched over in that golf cart. You talk about a fiasco... imagine three old men trying to do CPR on a dead guy.

Again, I felt completely calm, and again, I found myself observing the events as they continued in the natural world. I was about ten feet above the cart, and as I watched the commotion below, I became aware of an intense presence behind me on my right side.

Turning towards the source of this presence, I saw a large angel about nine feet tall absolutely radiating light. Instantly, I remembered that the being had also been present with me in the hospital room the last time my heart had stopped in 1982. I recalled its strong and serene countenance. It certainly knew who I was.

Looking at the angel, I understood that this time I would not be given a choice to go back, and that my life was now over. Its thoughts, its words, were instantly conveyed to me so that I perfectly understood in both my mind and my heart what it was communicating. There would be no misunderstanding in this new realm.

"Jim," the angel said. "I am here at the request of God the Almighty Father, through the intercession of the Holy Spirit, by way of the Sacrifice of His Most Victorious Son,

Jesus Christ. I am here to take you Home. You will need to stay close to me."

Immediately, I began to pray to God.

———

A nun once told me in school, Jimmy, that not all of the angels in the Bible have wings. But this one most certainly did. The sound of those wings lifting us off the ground was something I had never heard in all my years of flight. It was as if each feather was an instrument playing in a complex symphony that erupted as soon as we took off. We rose up over the trees and I looked back one last time at the scene below me.

My consciousness, in fact all of my thoughts and memories, were the same as they were just minutes before… yet I felt more alive than ever. I smiled to myself knowing that I had certainly just ruined the guys' round of golf.

My life on Earth was finished, and I thought about your mother. I also thought about you and your siblings, Jimmy. The world below me was now spinning away, as we rose through the atmosphere and into the stars above….

— 4 —
KOREA, 1951

It was 1951, and I would be leaving you, your mother, your brother and your sister in just a few short weeks. Your youngest brother, Mark, hadn't been born yet. I will tell you why he came close to having never been born at all. You were only five years old, and I had been notified that I was being called up to fight in the Korean War.

I was in the Air Force Reserves. Being in the Reserves gave our family an extra paycheck, and I was able to keep flying planes at our local base. However, I didn't think that weekend warriors like me would be called in first to stop the growing threat of Communism in the Far East. Nevertheless, I was going; and on a weekend in September before I left, our young family headed down to the Lake of the Ozarks to spend some time together. We attended an Air Force sendoff party thrown for the families of the officers in our squadron.

The weekend was difficult to enjoy because it was little more than a military function. All I could think about was heading back to war, knowing how many times I had come close to being shot down in World War II.

Were my reflexes still as good at twenty-eight as they had been at twenty-one? Could I still make split-second decisions and make the correct calculations like I did when I was flying every day in 1944? I knew there were younger pilots who could have been sent before our Reservists, but Uncle Sam was calling up the veterans instead of the rookies.

Now that I had a wife, three kids, and a career selling life insurance, I had moved on with my life. My thoughts became consumed with heading back to war and being alone again inside that cockpit. At the end of the Saturday night dinner held that weekend, I looked at your mother, and then at you, and then at Denny and Peggy. In disgust, I pushed myself away from the table and yanked loose my necktie. Your mother quietly asked me to calm down. I told her I didn't care if anyone noticed my frustration or not.

After having already flown six years earlier in World War II, they were calling me up ahead of the younger pilots who hadn't seen any combat at all. I was angry, but, in all fairness, I was scared to leave my family, Jimmy.

I know your mom was scared, too, because my deployment was to last a year. To reassure her, I told her that other officers were saying the Korean warfront was not as dangerous as what we had faced in Europe. Rumors circulated among the pilots that the "milk runs" in Korea were nothing like our combat missions in Germany.

I hoped the rumors were true.

———

October, 1951, I arrived at the United Nations base in Won Ju, South Korea. The Air Force had awarded me my "Certificate of Proficiency" earlier that August when I had completed my advanced fighter training in Arizona, and I was technically now a specialist in the F-51 Fighter Combat Crew. I was assigned to fly a Mustang with my new group, the 67th Fighter Squadron.

The F-51 Mustangs were fast and they were loud; Mustangs were mean machines with a mouthful of teeth painted on a few of their noses. I no longer wore the vulture of the 367th Squadron on my flight jacket. Instead, my new insignia bore the image of the 67th's boxing rooster.

The main job of the 67th was to break up the enemy supply lines feeding the North Korean army, whose railroads and tunnels zigzagged across the mountainous terrain. Our pilots carried flight maps detailed for every mission, and we were able to pinpoint the Communist targets in the topography beneath us.

On my first mission, we attacked enemy naval bases along Wonson Beach, on the Eastern Korean shore of the Sea of Japan. I called your mother after that first mission and told her not to worry. So far so good, and the anti-aircraft fire that the North Koreans threw at us was nothing like what we had faced against the Germans. The guys on base were a relaxed group, and I got along well with the other pilots.

The next morning, October 27, we reviewed the flight plan for the attack we would be making on some North Korean supply facilities later that afternoon. We had been briefed that our targets were to make rail cuts on a section of tracks near Kunu-ri, and then continue north and destroy routes around the town of Yongdong-ni.

We took off around 1:00 in the afternoon, flying across the 38th Parallel separating North and South Korea. Less than two hours later, we arrived at the target. I was the second plane in the lead flight, and as we approached, I lined up and salvoed my four rockets. I pulled off the target in a skidding turn, took spacing, and then made a second pass hitting the enemy infrastructure again with my guns.

Just as I began my pull-up, I saw a soldier shooting at me from the top of a hill outside the town. It seemed like slow motion as I looked him right in the eye… he pointed his handgun at my aircraft, and fired.

Suddenly, I felt the impact of a small explosion below my feet on the underside of my aircraft. Heavy black smoke filled the cockpit almost immediately, making it impossible to read my instruments—I also lost reference to my position in relationship to the ground. I ducked my head and jettisoned the canopy, hoping that would allow me to see clearly. The smoke was so thick, Jimmy.

Even as I called my flight leader, stating that I had been hit and was in trouble, I was pulling the aircraft up into a steep climb. I lowered full flaps and banked to the right. I still could not see, so I took off my helmet and oxygen hose and unlocked the safety belt, preparing to bail.

However, the belt got stuck and I couldn't get out, Jimmy. It was dark and I was packed to the gills with equipment and the seatbelt was stuck. My plane had always been my fortress, but, now when I needed to get out of her, I couldn't.

No longer could I slow her down as the plane approached a stall, smoking and in flames. I had to eject, so I reached down under my legs to try and free the belt. Suddenly, I popped loose and I tell you, Jimmy, if I was ever born again it was right then. Rolling out, I tucked myself as the slip-stream threw me backwards; the tail surface slicing by only about five or six feet above my head.

I must have left the aircraft at about 2,000 feet. Spinning like a top, I eventually steadied into a controlled fall and grabbed my rip cord. After deploying and opening my chute, I observed the plane, trailing smoke, hit the ground exploding about a mile from the Main Supply Route. Coming down, I could see no enemy activity around me, and you can bet I liked it that way.

I knew I was exposed as I floated through the sky. Feeling the wind in my hair, all I could think about was protecting my head when I landed. Even though I was anticipating my approach, I struck the ground on a slight downhill slope, bouncing hard and skidding to a stop.

Despite the adrenaline rushing through me, I could tell I was hurt. I would later learn that the impact tore ligaments in both my left knee and right ankle.

The roar of the other Mustangs from the 67th Squadron filled the sky above me. My flight leader was already giving me cover, so after I had released the parachute harness and pinned it to the ground with my trench knife, I waved to let him know I was okay.

My next step, actually my next crawl, was to pull out my .45, charge it and lay it on the ground. I then opened my backpack escape kit which contained my radio. After assembling it, I checked in with the flight leader, Captain

Anderson, who was capping me. He assured me that one of the lads in the flight was already summoning the rescue copter team, and told me to stay there and relax. I followed the first part of his instructions.

Next, I unpacked the escape kit, filling my pockets with any items I thought necessary. I had learned long before, as a kid in the Boy Scouts, to always be prepared.

The guys on base used to give me static because I laid out all of my issued survival equipment each night before my flights. I had it all on me, and on every combat mission: shark repellent, marker dye, carbine bayonet trench knife, pocket knife, pen knife, .45 caliber pistol and clip, shoulder holster, 'Mae West' flotation device, dog tags, currency, Korean-English dictionary, small bartering kit, compass, flint fire starter, mechanical pencil, fountain pen, flashlight, silk scarf, handkerchief (for filtering water), map, life raft, United Nations I.D., URC-4 radio, flares, matches, Zippo lighter, pack of cigarettes, mirror, compass, extra pair of socks, backpack, wrist watch, wool hat, leather gloves, wedding ring and a medal cross around my neck. Those gabardine flight suits had a place for just about everything, and you can bet I filled up each pocket just in case I ever needed any of it.

I realized that because of my legs, I would have to be picked up by the copter before nightfall, or face capture.

Spreading out my chute, I stuck my three knives in it to hold so that the helicopter would be better able to spot me. I then crawled to a ditch and prepared for a wait by laying out my cigarettes, lighter, .45 and radio. I notified the cover flight that they were drawing automatic weapon fire from the north, and advised them to make orbit farther to the south. There were still two fighters circling above and covering me.

Locking my radio and setting it in the receive position, I heard all conversations and soon learned that two enemy soldiers were attempting to reach me. I tried not to think of the stories I had heard of pilots being taken prisoner by the Communists.

My cover aircraft fired a warning burst in front of the two men, but both continued to advance on my position. The aircraft made another pass and again fired a warning burst. I called and told the fellas not to strafe all over the place, as I might have to live with these people for a long time. The fellas must have been sure I was going to be rescued because they set up a traffic pattern on the area. On the next pass, one man retreated and the other was claimed KIA.

I heard the radio calls between the copter and its cover flight. Four more Mustangs rushed towards my position, making a rocket pass to the northwest of me; followed again with several strafing attacks to prevent more automatic fire. I tell you, Jimmy, those Mustangs showed up to save a fellow downed pilot, and they meant business.

I called and suggested the helicopter make its approach from the southeast after the jets did their best to clear the area. The copter came into view, and seeing those blades miraculously appear out of the smoke was a sight I will never forget.

The helicopter made three passes toward my position, but each time as it approached to within thirty or forty yards, the enemy fire increased tremendously and the copter was forced to withdraw. I heard the pilot say he thought the area was too hot to make a successful pick-up and that he would have to leave. Of course, I disagreed with his opinion. I started to call in on the radio but heard the Lieutenant interrupt—ordering the Mustangs to quiet down the area so that the helicopter pilot could stand by for just one more pass.

With this, I was entirely in accord. So was the pilot of the copter, provided I left the immediate area. The rescue pilot wanted me to run to the southeast about 200 yards... or at least as far as I could. This was the last attempt. The Mustangs began strafing the entire area, on all sides of me, just as the copter began to lose altitude for the final approach.

As the fighters roared in, I ran like an injured gazelle in the direction of the copter's pass.

Enemy ground fire opened up again as the copter and I approached head-to-head. The copter was still moving when I grabbed the metal bar used for carrying litters. I hung on to the skiff and the corpsman in the copter hung on to me. Aided by the medic and strongly motivated by all the shooting around me, I crawled in before we had gained even a few hundred feet.

We got out of there at dusk, just as the sun was setting on that awful place.

———

Jimmy, it took the nerve of people like that helicopter pilot, and the other guys covering me, to get men back. There were those who were not as fortunate as I was, and the only reason I ever made it back home to you and our family was because of the selfless acts of that cover team, who refused to give up.

Our helicopter made it back to base without further event and they unloaded me off the deck. I was taken to the hospital for X-rays and treatment. When the medical staff had determined that there was nothing wrong with me other than a couple of torn ligaments, I was discharged and transferred to Japan for rehab. This completed my second, and last, mission with the 67th Fighter Bomber Squadron.

In Japan, I figured the only way I could fully recuperate was to go play golf. I played a little bit and got better. Once the Air Force saw that I was able to fly again, they put me back to work piloting a big carrier plane transporting troops between the Korean peninsula and Japan. Remarkably, I still enjoyed flying even after everything that had happened... but I was ready to go home.

Do you remember my homecoming Jimmy, with the big picnic in the park? I brought you and Denny each a red and black silk jacket, and you guys thought you were something else. We floated those little hand-carved, Japanese toy boats in the pond together. I remember you kept staring at the red mustache I had grown, and you didn't like it much! It was amazing to be back, and to see your sister, you boys, and your mother again. What a thing to look at your faces knowing where I had been, just a few months before.

It was surreal to be back home, Jimmy, back in our apartment on Plaza Drive. Sometimes, at night after falling asleep next to your mom in bed, I would wake up—gasping, choking, trapped again in that smoking plane.

— 5 —
LEAVING *this* WORLD

As the angel and I went up through the clouds, I knew we were traveling at a faster speed than I had ever flown while piloting in the skies over Earth. The color of the sky, once we broke through the atmosphere, went from light blue, to cobalt, to the deep black of space as we entered eternity.

It was thrilling to look down and see the same planet I had just left. From the mountains and oceans to the continents now circling below me, I recognized that the familiar features of our Earth actually existed in this new realm, too. And yet, here I was, traveling with an angel of God, becoming aware of so much more.

After my bailout in 1951, I told your mom that I was done flying. Yet, I kept up with current events, fascinated that some of the guys I read about had entered the space program. John Glenn had flown in both World War II and the Korean War during the same years that I had flown. He went on to pilot supersonic jets and made headlines with NASA. I always wondered what kept guys like that so hungry.

Yet, here I was, orbiting the Earth without even so much as an aircraft around me. I felt a renewed passion and excitement, a sense of wonder—I was freed from the constraints of physics, once again, thanks to flight...

I was a young man again, Jimmy.

As we traveled deep into space, I realized I no longer needed to breathe. At the same time, all of my senses had become intensified. I could feel the rush of movement around my new spiritual body. I looked over at the angel, who was wearing a golden sash around its white robe, and I knew that the being had been my guardian throughout my entire life. The angel looked at me and told me its name was Glale; that's the best way I can spell the name. When the angel had pronounced, "Glale," it sounded more like the ringing of a bell.

The stars were everywhere now—millions of galaxies and solar systems shone as far as I could see. Just as I was beginning to ponder all of this, two more angels arrived, moving at a tremendous velocity, accelerating alongside our flanks.

Our party had now grown to four. We were traveling in what I knew to be a "Finger-Four" formation: one of the new angels took its position on the far left, in the 'first finger' position, Glale took the flight lead in the 'middle finger' position, I was in the third 'ring finger' position, and the fourth angel was to my right-rear, or in the 'little finger' position. It was clear that the two outside angels were there for my protection—I guess you could call them my wingmen, and I looked at the two, curiously.

Then Glale said to me, "Jim, it is written in the Book of Exodus, 'See, I am sending an angel ahead of you to guard you along the way and to bring you to the place I have prepared'" (Exodus 23:20).

Thinking it was an odd way to start a conversation, I didn't reply. However, the stars were beginning to dim, and the atmosphere in which we were moving through now felt... heavy.

The darkness around us was palpable. After the angel had said its words to me, I was suddenly filled with a sense of dread.

Off in the distance, I now heard screams.

———

Jimmy, when I was a kid, I can remember feeling sick, or falling down and hurting myself. My dad would tell me to offer up my small sufferings "for the souls in Purgatory." I know I said the same thing to you once or twice.

But now, I found myself moving through a void and hearing the most terrible wailing I had ever heard. The sound was horrifying. It was coming far off from one side of us, and these screams were worse than anything I had witnessed from either of my times in the war hospitals.

Mentally, I must have wondered to myself if we were close to Purgatory. "As Christ spoke regarding the sheep and the goats (Matthew 25:31), there is but Heaven and Hell," came the response from Glale.

In the story of Lazarus and the rich man, Christ described a great chasm by which none could freely enter nor escape the prison of Hell (Luke 16:19). That chasm was now off to our right.

I didn't want to learn more. Fear seemed to be all around. I didn't want to stop, and I prayed that we would hurry past....

— 6 —
MARCH 22, 1968

It was hard to leave my parents in 1942 when I joined the Army. It was even harder to leave you when I was sent to Korea in 1951. However, after you were drafted in 1968, driving you downtown to the Army induction center and seeing you get on that bus to Fort Leonard Wood was the hardest day of all.

We muttered a few words to each other in that big hall. Then, you asked me for some advice on what you should do when you got to Vietnam.

So many thoughts flashed through my mind: don't try and be a hero, don't make yourself a target; on breaks, at least have a cigarette in your hand so they don't make you clean the johns. There was a lot of wisdom I could have imparted to a new recruit like you that day.

Instead, I replied, "You'll do fine."

That was it. I'm sure you remember. I'm sorry that I hadn't done better for you that day, and I wish I would have told you that I love you.

I wanted to tell you that stepping off that plane and landing in a war zone at the age of twenty-two would be the loneliest feeling in the world. Imagining you in that situation was too much for me, and the last thing you needed that day was me falling apart. As I'm sure you've experienced a few times as a parent, sometimes a dad is just trying to keep it together himself.

I thought about all of my military decorations sitting upstairs in a shoebox: the Distinguished Flying Cross, the Purple Heart, the Air Medals. None of them were doing me any good now. During the Vietnam draft, everyone was trying to run for the exits. The truth was that I was proud of you, Jimmy. I was also scared for you, just as your mother was, and there was nothing else I could do other than try and encourage you.

You had already finished college, and it would be to your advantage to be one of the older and more experienced guys in your platoon. All your life you were such a good boy and such a good example for your younger siblings; they looked up to you. I really believed in you, too, Jimmy—I knew you had a good head on your shoulders, and I knew the Army would prepare you as much as they could before you were deployed.

But war is unpredictable, as you now know.

I read the papers and I watched the news that year while you were overseas. It made your mother and me so anxious that we often had to turn off the TV. I have been in wars, and I have had a son in war, and I would have chosen the former any day of the week.

In the 1940s, my parents would read the headlines from the warfront, and read about the great heroics of the boys overseas. In 1968 and 1969, your mom and I had to read about the protests and the politicians. It made me mad, and it made your mother even madder. You deserved better from your country.

———

When you were a kid, Jimmy, I would take you over to the Northside YMCA where we all played handball. The guys loved seeing you, Jimmy. Of course, it wasn't a very kid-friendly place. Your mom disliked the Y.

As you may remember, most of the guys down there were veterans of the foreign wars, too. We hung out, drank beer, and competed against each other. The Y was great. That's why a few of us later formed the Hinder Club downtown in the old Armory building, because we all loved playing handball and being together.

I was pretty outgoing and thrived off the interaction with the other guys. It also helped me stay in contact with my friends and colleagues, which was important to someone selling life insurance. As you kids grew up and had families of your own, you and your brothers played a lot of handball at the Hinder Club, too. You were all great players.

You were able to blow off some steam there, as well. But, I knew that you always put your family first, and spent most of your free time at home. I respected you for that.

When my generation returned home, we were celebrated. Many of us still carried the war with us, and although most of us didn't openly talk about it, we were able to bond knowing that we had all made it through somehow. I was able to leave some of what I wrestled with there on the handball courts, or in the locker room, or at the clubhouse poker table on the weekends.

The country changed, and by the time you returned home in 1969, no one was there to give you boys anything but the cold shoulder. I saw how it affected you.

You veterans of Vietnam shouldered a cross, and it was heavy. My generation was celebrated, and we never had to feel your pain.

Jimmy, I didn't have the right words for you when you left for Vietnam. And I didn't have the right words for you when you came back, either. But the Lord of Heaven knows what it feels like to serve and get spit on in return.

Please, just remember that they jeered at Him, too, Jimmy. And He forgave them anyway.

— 7 —
ARRIVAL

The three angels and I moved through the darkness, and my fear intensified. The lead angel, Glale, turned to me mid-flight and said, "Do not fear, Jim, for the Lord has redeemed you through His most Holy Sacrifice. It is written that because of this gift, 'there is no condemnation for those who are in Christ, Jesus'" (Romans 8:1).

I would emphasize again, Jimmy, that we bring into the next world what we take with us from our earthly life. I'm not talking about physical things, but rather the gifts of the spirit. My personality, my experiences and my knowledge, were still with me after death and remained just as they were during my last moments on Earth. What I am saying is that the Word we carry in our hearts on Earth makes for a safer passage through death.

"In the beginning was the Word, and the Word was with God, and the Word was God" (John 1:1). When I read those words as a young man, I was changed. That is why I took the name James Joseph "John" as my Confirmation name.

In that moment with the angels, I better understood what John was saying: the Word is Alive, and it is both our safety in life, and in death. It is the very covenant that kept me safe, when I believed it in the darkness.

In the Psalms, King David may have walked through the valley of the shadow of death (Psalm 23:4).

Now, I had just flown right through it.

———

So many have avoided a similar path through the dark void of death, simply by surrendering totally and completely to God while on Earth, Jimmy. "If you declare with your mouth, 'Jesus is Lord,' and believe in your heart that God raised him from the dead, you will be saved" (Romans 10:9). When I understood and believed in the angel's words, that's the moment the Light appeared up ahead.

I recognized it once again from many years before in that hospital room. The Light grew in the distance, and as we approached, it intensified. As the Light became larger, I remembered what followed John's first verse: "The light shines in the darkness, and the darkness has not overcome it" (John 1:5).

The Light expanded and we were drawn completely into it. The last time I saw the Light, after my heart attack, God spoke to me as the Father. Yet, I had remained far off from its beauty. Now, I realized that this Light of God illuminated an entire new realm, shining with the brilliance of His eternal majesty.

In this radiant place, a world too bright for human eyes, everything was more vivid; it shone in an intense clarity. There were colors everywhere, Jimmy, as we moved through this realm. The Light expanded the spectrum to include hues that I had never before seen.

We were moving through clouds once again. The scene looked like a Renaissance fresco painted high above the altar of some European cathedral. Surrounding me were layers upon layers of clouds, like levels of glory, with heavenly beings moving above the highest billows.

Sound erupted all around us, with music and singing rhythmically melding together like anthems. Some of the melodies were songs I recognized from Earth. While I could discern separate harmonies, they were all blending together in a powerful arrangement of praise for God.

I was aware of a sweet fragrance. This scent was pleasant and infinite, like smelling a garden full of flowers on a spring day. Yet, a personality was attached to this scent... it was as if it were emanating from someone, or something, that I had always known.

———

My senses were totally engaged. I saw that we were approaching an enormous and fortified City, coming in from an altitude of what I estimated to be around 1,000 feet. We were high enough to see above the walls and into this brilliant City itself.

Surrounding the outside borders were mountains of an intensity and height that dwarfed the Rockies, Pyrenees, or any other range I had seen while piloting in the skies above Earth. These new mountains also had peaks glistening with snow, and I knew that snow meant atmosphere. The magnetic pull towards the center of the City suggested to me that we were approaching from a southwesterly direction.

Glale spoke, saying that many arrive into God's Kingdom through one of the twelve main gates within the enormous walls. Archangels guard each of the deep porticos. One must be vouched for by his or her guardian angel before entering; the guardian angel "stands in the gap," next to the human being whose life the guardian angel has witnessed. Next, the recording angel then checks the register, to see if

Upper Left:
James "Jim" Joseph McCabe
St. Louis University High School
Class of 1941.

Upper Right:
Jim and his sister, Nancy McCabe
in 1942. Nancy, once a Rockette in
her twenties, died during childbirth
in 1955 at the age of thirty-four.

Lower Right:
Jim and his father, Harry D. McCabe
in 1942. Jim left home at the age of
nineteen to join the Army after the
attack on Pearl Harbor.

Upper Right:
The wedding party of Mr. & Mrs.
James J. McCabe, St. Rose's Church,
November 18, 1944.

Lower Right:
Jim and Mary Wientge-McCabe
were high school sweethearts. They
were married for 49 years and had
four children together.

Lower Left:
Mary in 1944 on her honeymoon
with Jim in California.

Below:
Old St. Rose of Lima Catholic Church
Est. 1884 in St. Louis, MO.
Image © Chris Naffziger /
St. Louis Patina

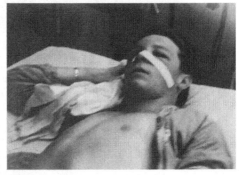

Upper Left:
Jim McCabe, Theodore Knickmeyer and another cadet at Randolph Field Training Center, Texas, 1942.

Middle Left:
Clipping from the St. Louis Star-Times, Aug. 24, 1942. Jim earned his wings and was sent for Advanced Training to be a fighter pilot.

Middle Right:
Jim McCabe in the Randolph Field Hospital after a training crash left another pilot dead. Sept. 17, 1942.

Lower Left:
Lt. Jim McCabe, Oct. 1943, England.

Brothers Fight In Same Raid Over Reich Without Knowing It

Two St. Louis brothers recently were reunited in the air over Germany, but they didn't realize it until later when they met—on the ground—in England.

ST.LOUIS POST-DISPATCH

Virginia Irwin Finds St. Louisans With 'Work Horse' P-47 Group

From left: CAPT. FRED L. HILLIS, CPL. ROBERT W. OBERSCHELP and LT. JAMES J. McCABE.

Thunderbirds' of Nineteenth Tactical Air Force Fly as Many as 23 Missions a Day in Support of Patton's Troops.

9/27/44

Upper Left:
Officer Jim McCabe in London, 1944.

Upper Right:
Newspaper headlines from the European Theater reporting on Jim's missions and "Work Horse" group, 1944.

Middle Left:
Flight footage from Lt. McCabe's combat film, April 25, 1941. In this frame the 367th Squadron was attacking ground targets in Germany.

Middle Right and Bottom Right:
Jim McCabe and his P-47 Thunderbolt, the "Lil' Pecker."

Below images:
*Artistic renderings of Capt. Jim McCabe's Evasion & Escape Report Oct. 27, 1951 in the Korean War.
Images © Tim McCabe / youtube.com/watch?v=Wg3sIVLISOA*

Captain Jim McCabe next to his F-51 Mustang;
United Nations Air Base, Won Ju, South Korea, 1951.

ST. LOUIS PILOT TELLS OF RESCUE IN KOREA

Capt. James J. McCabe Picked Up by Helicopter From Behind Red Lines.

Capt. James J. McCabe, back home in St. Louis after 11 months as a fighter pilot in Korea, gave details yesterday of his hairbreadth rescue last October by helicopter after being shot down behind Communist lines.

"I was piloting an F-51 Mustang fighter-bomber, dive-bombing a railroad line and some troop billets in North Korea when anti-aircraft fire struck the plane," he related. "The plane caught fire, but I was able to crash land.

Capt. McCabe.

St. Louis Post-Dispatch article
detailing Jim's rescue, 1952.

Left:
Jim's oldest brother, Captain Harry "Don" McCabe. Don was a B-24 Liberator pilot and co-pilot. Don unknowingly flew alongside Jim on a bombing raid into Germany in 1944.

Right:
Jim's second oldest brother, Bill, a radio operator during the war.

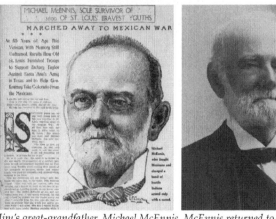

Jim's great-grandfather, Michael McEnnis. McEnnis returned to St. Louis after serving several months in New Mexico in the Mexican-American War. He was sent home to attend to his family in 1849, and put in charge of burying victims of the cholera epidemic.
Above Left: *Image courtesy of Newspapers.com/St. Louis Post Dispatch, May 14, 1911*
Above Right: *Image courtesy of the Missouri Historical Society*

Above: Cannons at Fort McHenry, Maryland, used during the War of 1812. George McNeir, grandfather of Michael McEnnis, was Commander of the Sea Fencibles during the Battle of Baltimore.
Image © Joseph Sohm / Shutterstock

Left:
Jim returned home from Korea in 1952 to his wife and three children.

Top Right:
Jim on vacation in the 1950s with his children Jimmy, Denny, and Peggy. Jim and Mary's fourth child, Mark, would be born in 1955.

Bottom Right:
Jim's wife, Mary, and their four children in 1958.

Mary and Jim McCabe, pictured with two of their grandchildren, Mike and Tim, in 1980.

Clockwise from Left:
Jim McCabe Sr., Jim "Jimmy" McCabe Jr., and the author in 1991.

James "Jim" Joseph John McCabe died on the golf course, August 19, 1993.

the person's name has been written in blood in the Lamb's Book of Life (Rev 13:8). When the name is verified, that person is escorted into Heaven to the cheers of millions of God's people, and to the sounds of a hundred thousand trumpets.

As the angel spoke this, the music grew louder, filling the air around us. The seraphim, who worship God eternally in the highest places, circled in the clouds above and their praises filled the sky. Suddenly, Glale and I dropped down lower towards the City walls.

The two angels who had previously joined us, now shot forward and flew towards an archangel stationed on one of the wall towers. The archangel nodded at us, and then made a signal with its arm.

A roar erupted below. I saw millions of people in white, looking up and praising God when they saw that we had been cleared to enter the airspace. The sky changed colors as if made from a rainbow, and the musical and visual harmony was like some kind of masterfully orchestrated symphony.

Over and over, the crowd of saints sang, "Seek ye first the kingdom of God, and His righteousness!" Other angelic beings, further outside the City's perimeter, joined the singing in unison. The City pulsated with colors, and the perfect organization of the millions of buildings and incredible architecture was unique to anything built on Earth. There were great halls, courtyards and chalets... open plazas and gardens. Crystalline rivers flowed, running though the City, erupting in fountains and spilling in measured designs. Somehow, the City's precise planning added to the glory of the scene, as mansions, villas, and dwellings were all arranged in a perfect vertical and horizontal cohesion.

Paradoxically, the City was enormous, yet seemed so intimate. I felt like we could be anywhere in an instant, unlimited by time and space. Although I stuck close to Glale, I was free to move by my own accord, gliding left and right, enjoying the atmosphere that was of the perfect temperature.

I maintained the same five senses that I had possessed while on Earth. Yet, each sense was magnified by the exciting sights, sounds, smells and physical sensations that I was experiencing with my new spiritual body.

At last, I finally felt like I had come home....

— 8 —
MARY ROSE

I met your mother when we were in high school. We were young, and we happened to be opposites: I liked to tell jokes, and she was shy; I went to private school, and she went to public school. We were always a good fit.

After I left for World War II, she wrote me often while I was stationed in England. Isn't it funny how two young kids can end up spending a whole lifetime with each other? We got married, had children, and went through all of life's ups and downs together, and I couldn't have asked for someone better with whom to share those experiences.

It was a pretty traditional marriage in our house. I worked many years for the insurance company, while she stayed home with all of you. Yet, your mom was strong and we complimented each other well. She instilled great values in you. Your mom was a dependable person, and I loved her very much.

After we got married in 1944, we took a little honeymoon while I was on leave. Even though it was only a short tour out West, we had a blast.

During my earthly life, people used to tell me that I had a tendency to give others the benefit of the doubt... even when it was clear the other party was being disingenuous. My father was like that, too. He had a generous heart. But, the amount of compassion and patience your mother showed me over the years was a constant reminder that people are always a work in progress.

Altogether, your mother and I were married for almost fifty years. We made it to year forty-nine before I died on the golf course. I would have really liked to celebrate our fiftieth anniversary together.

You remember Mr. Gilmore from our handball club, right? He was a day younger than me, and we had been lifelong friends. Our lives followed a similar path ever since we were teenagers. He knew how often I had come close to dying over the years, yet *his* health towards the end of our lives was even worse than mine. That fat old man was the same guy who had once gotten his parachute caught on a church steeple during the D-Day invasion—he had been with the Airborne Rangers, and he was a tough old bird.

Mr. Gilmore and I had a running bet as to who would live longer. Of course, whoever died first, lost the bet. Each year on my birthday, he would pay me a dollar because I had technically made it to the next milestone. Then, the next day,

I'd pay him the dollar back. Mr. Gilmore died before me, and that son-of-a-gun never paid up.

Your mother disliked Mr. Gilmore and I getting together for our annual squaring of the deal. She thought our talk was morbid and ghoulish. But Mr. Gilmore and I found our birthdays to be a cause for great celebration. We'd go up the street to the tavern each year, and sometimes I'd even bring your little brother, Mark, with me. Your mom disliked that, too.

What a happy house we had, Jimmy. That's how your mom and I always remembered it. I was harder on you than the other three, of course. Your mom used to remind me of that, when you and I would get frustrated with each other.

Ultimately, your mom and I just wanted the best for you. When you were a young man and came back from the war, you would always swing by and put a few extra bucks in your little brother's wallet or top off the gas in your sister's car. Looking back, I wish I had taken more opportunities to just observe your strong character. Because, as I can attest to now, it really is character that counts in the end.

— 9 —

The LODGE

Flying over the vibrant City, I attempted to take it all in. It was enormous. Glale reminded me of the words the Lord spoke in John 14:2, "My Father's house has many dwellings; if that were not so, would I have told you that I am going there to prepare a place for you?"

There were indeed many, many dwellings here. I wanted to stop and look inside them all, but we were moving at too fast a pace. Clearly, my angel and I were heading somewhere else, and I was really excited to get there.

The houses began thinning out, and there was more green space between the homes as we moved outside of the City. Mentally, I thought of this new area as the "suburbs" of Heaven. There were parks, paths, gazebos, tall monuments and bridges over the clear flowing streams.

Pools and rivers that sourced from the main River of Life now rushed wildly throughout the countryside. Animals grazed everywhere in the fields below. We soared over thickening woodlands and open meadows, as the roar of the living waters grew louder.

Following one of the rivers, we came to a raging waterfall that rushed over the edge of a drop-off—and we suddenly swooped down into the most scenic valley I had ever seen.

The expanse that lay in front of us was filled with rolling hills and mountains beyond, covered in a carpet of a million green treetops. From our vantage point, the valley looked like the forests I had seen on Earth, full of leafy deciduous trees and occasional tall evergreen groves on the higher ridges.

Colorful songbirds flew around the canopy below, as we sped along, shooting above the unlimited forests.

———

As we followed the river that thundered through this verdant landscape, Glale cruised down to just above the treetops. He turned slightly towards the right, and we began flying in what I discerned to be a more southeasterly direction.

Once again, I started seeing amazing homes. Many were built into the hilltops, and others, like tree-mansions perched in the canopy heights. I saw a house that literally rose out of the middle of the roiling river, half below the water, half above. An ornate bridge, made of buttresses carved with rich stonework, connected the house to the bank. More monuments, courtyards, parks, gardens and banquet halls dotted the clearings.

We slowed down as we came to a high, lush dome. Speeding along its contour, we arrived at a large open space on top of the promontory, with several beautiful structures situated towards the edges of the grounds.

It wasn't until my feet touched the soft lawn that I remembered just how terrifying it is to land from a high altitude back on Earth. This time, there were no twisted ankles or ripped knees, only the forgiving carpet of rich grass beneath my feet.

The angel alighted on the ground, too, and looked out at the valley below. For the first time, I took a long look at this Glale. The angel was huge, and powerful, and those wings were shimmering white. I'm not sure, but I think I sensed a bit of relief on the angel's face. It must have witnessed a lot, having followed me around for seventy years.

———

I stared at the angel, and then I recalled a moment that I hadn't thought of in many years.

1943... up over the English Channel on an escort mission... inclement weather was approaching on the radar. This wasn't unusual as we were always battling the choppy currents of the Channel. Air Control radioed in that our group should return to base because of the approaching storm. So, we all pulled up, and turned back.

A call like that in the sky from Air Control was a good one. I took my time and eased off the throttle, rocking my wings a bit, testing the air and banking into some clouds just for fun. I decided I really wasn't that eager to get back to base, so I started monkeying around, dipping and diving through the clouds.

In flight school they had taught us that the odds of ever surviving a "flat spin" in one of those heavy fighters was slim to none. Our instructors had shown us footage of a plane devolving into a spin, spiraling like the hands of a clock before crashing into the surface below.

I saw a cloud bank and popped into it. As soon as I dropped down, I was sucked into a flat spin.

It was frightening. The plane was whipping in circles, plummeting towards the ocean as it lost altitude. The centrifugal force pinned me to the side of the cockpit—it seemed like my plane would hit the water at any moment. Knowing I was in trouble, I jumped on my pedal as hard as I could.

And then my plane righted itself, and I regained control. Just like that.

Had this angel been there with me on that rainy day over the English Channel? Had this angel been there with me my entire life?

I wondered about the times when I had suffered, or when I had sinned. Had this angel left me? When Satan tempted Christ, many angels came and attended to Jesus *after* the devil had left Him (Matthew 4:11). What about the boys in the war whose planes had actually gone down? Weren't their angels flying alongside them, too? Could an angel be beaten? What kind of horrible demon could inflict damage on a mighty warrior like this Glale?

Why had I survived the war?

Why had my angel kept me safe, when other young men had died so tragically?

Why did God send me back after my heart had stopped at fifty-nine years old?

Where in this Heaven was I now?

"Jim!"

As I stood looking at the angel and at the panorama around me, I heard a voice to my right, and so I turned. That's when I saw her. She was radiant, Jimmy. Smiling, just the same as I remembered her. She ran to me and we hugged. It was my sister, Nancy.

Don and Bill were older than Nancy and I. In age, she was my closest sibling, and she always "mothered" me. When I started smoking in the fifth grade, I worried that Nancy would catch me smoking just as much as if my mother would catch me.

Nancy was quiet, humble, and always smiling. However, she also took it upon herself to keep me in line. There's a picture in one of our old photo albums of Nancy and me right after I joined the Army. I had come home for a few days and I was wearing my new uniform, feeling pretty good about myself. In that old photo I am saying something and laughing, and Nancy is looking at me, smiling. A gifted dancer herself, having even once performed in New York with the Rockettes, Nancy often stayed in the background while her brothers took home all the accolades.

Nancy died when she was thirty-four, and I was heartbroken. Your mom loved being around Nancy, too, as they had known each other for years.

Now here she was, and here I was. I didn't even know what to say to her. We just smiled at each other, and it was like we were suddenly kids again.

Eventually I asked her, "Where am I?"

She laughed and said, "Welcome to the Lodge!"

I looked around. The scenery was breathtaking. Even the pathway behind Nancy, leading through the landscaping and towards the buildings, was intricately crafted. This was all a far cry from the woody hills of the Midwest. I smiled and said, "I don't understand."

———

Jimmy, if you recall, our family going to the Ozarks a few times. It was close enough to our house for a weekend getaway, and you and your siblings always liked going out on the boat or playing in the creeks. We had some great times as a family there when you were younger.

You've seen the old pictures: photos with you and your brothers and sisters smiling and fishing. I'm in the background of some of the pictures... I'm the dad with the furrowed brow.

Our times at any of our few vacation destinations were always too short and too rushed, don't you think? I recall tensing up on Saturday nights, already dreading the trip back on Sunday morning. It meant getting up... packing... driving several hours... knowing I would be waking up early on Monday morning and heading back to my office in the Laclede Building. When I arrived at the office, I would regret having tried to fit a family trip in, and felt rushed trying to stay on top of my commissions.

Yet I loved our trips and now I wish we would have taken more, Jimmy. As you well know, a father is often trying to balance his home life with work. It's just how it goes. Eventually, you stop working, but by then there are no more little voices laughing and running around your home, and you wish for those days back again.

These are not new thoughts; I had thought these exact things while I was still on Earth, too. I remember getting ready to come home after a weekend on a family trip together. Between the rush of getting everyone packed, I was daydreaming, imagining the vacation I wished had existed instead. A place where time stood still, where I might be surrounded by loved ones and nature without any looming deadlines... and yes, a place that actually had clean, clear water, instead of the cloudy puddles where we swam.

Had Nancy heard my thoughts? Did Nancy know what I had subconsciously wished for during that short family trip back on Earth?

Looking down, I saw that we were standing on a footpath. It was intricately crafted... stunning to observe, as my eyes followed it. Inlaid with rocks, the path appeared to be made with some kind of mineralized gemstones. It led through the lawns and up to something that looked like an incredible clubhouse. Did this massive property belong entirely to her?

"Come on, Jim!" she said. "I have waited so long to show you this place."

———

Nancy was diagnosed with a brain tumor in May, 1955, while pregnant. She died in September. She refused the limited chemotherapy available at the time in order to protect her baby. Doctors kept Nancy alive long enough to ensure a safe delivery, and Nancy passed away just a few minutes after her daughter was delivered.

Perhaps you remember this, Jimmy. You were ten years old when she died. I remembered it all quite clearly, from my limited earthly perspective as her brother.

Now, outside this Lodge, Nancy walked next to me and told me what had happened from the perspective of Heaven, on the day that she died on Earth.

Christ once said, "Greater love has no one than this: to lay down one's life for one's friends" (John 15:13). At the moment Nancy died and her baby Kathleen was safely delivered, a great creative force exploded throughout God's Kingdom. Our Father blessed everything at once because Nancy had blessed the Lord with her selfless act.

The heavens were rejoicing at this act of love on Earth, just as the angels and saints rejoice whenever we boldly live in Christ. Yet this explosion of love actually left a trail of *construction* across the universe: God is a Creator. His Son is a Carpenter. Nancy told me that when she passed away, whoever had blessed Nancy during her life on Earth, was instantly blessed in Heaven... whether they had arrived yet or not. Treasures were given to her family and friends. Castles and manors were instantly founded throughout eternity for anyone who had ever loved Nancy.

She told me this property was all mine. She told me I actually had many other homes in Heaven that I had not yet seen; but this estate was a gift from her. "You ought to see my place," she said with a smile.

In Revelation 14:13, John states, "Our righteous deeds on earth will not be forgotten, but will follow us to heaven." Nancy's righteous deeds followed her to Heaven, and now I was being rewarded for them, too.

I told Nancy I had hardly "blessed" her on Earth. If anything, as a kid I might have cursed her a few times under my breath. Nancy cared for me... and in return, I often did whatever I wanted instead.

But Nancy replied, "I loved you, and you were such a good boy, Jim."

We walked along the path, and now I looked at my surroundings differently. Everything around us was personalized—for me. I don't know why I kept staring at that footpath... at the gorgeous craftsmanship of its inlaid stonework. Rustic, natural minerals, were set in a fascinating arrangement that captured my attention.

In the Holy City, through which the angel and I had just flown, the streets were paved with solid gold. Here, the stonework and landscaping around us took on the aesthetics of some royal country estate. I knew I had seen flint stones with patterns like these rocks in earthly creek beds. However, the Lord's mines in Heaven produced gems richer than anything quarried from the oldest mountains on Earth. Our Creator takes care that the roads and surfaces we walk on in Heaven are perfectly crafted.

Jimmy, can you imagine the way the Apostles' feet must have looked, and the horrible smell when they took off their sandals? Yet, He bent down and washed those feet (John 13:6). The ground in Heaven is clean, not filthy like on Earth; it is amazingly manicured, and we get to walk on that holy ground. Nancy and I leisurely walked along this incredible path, and eventually we arrived at the huge, wooden front doors of the Lodge.

Jimmy, the building materials in Heaven are not like the materials on Earth. Before I was deployed to Korea, I was flying in Arizona, doing some of my training over the petrified forests in the Southwest. I saw the fossilized tree trunks strewn about, transformed into impenetrable stone long ago. Now imagine two immense wood doors, hewn to display their ancient and gnarled features, the rich reds and purple wooden knots that had been treated and hardened by eternity. Other sparkling minerals were imbedded in the paneling, and the door handles were made of polished bronze.

Obviously, the One who had fashioned these doors knew trees—and woodworking. Looking around at the forests surrounding us, I recognized some of the trees from back on Earth. Many, however, were brand new to me. Nancy informed me that the doors were made from the wood of an American Chestnut, an extinct species on Earth. This was the specific wood the Lord chose to mark the entrance into my country estate.

I stood next to Nancy admiring the masterful woodcraft...

And then, the doors began to slowly open...

——

It is a good thing I had left that old, weak heart of mine behind because it wouldn't have stood a chance surviving what I now beheld in front of me.

Jimmy, all those who had once loved me and had already died on Earth were there now—waiting for me in that great hall. If they weren't in the hall, they were down playing golf in the valley below. I could see them through the huge glass windows lining the great room. My mother and my father were right there, and Thank God, it felt so good to hug them again.

"Welcome home!" my father said. He looked younger and happier than I recall seeing him on Earth. My mother was beaming, and looked beautiful. They were no longer carrying the pain from their lost savings in the Depression that affected them their whole lives.

Excited as I was to see them, my mom and dad were ecstatic to see me walk through that door. Can you imagine the excitement from their point of view? They say up here, getting to greet your own child in God's majestic Kingdom is the only thing better than having made it here yourself. I know the same will be true for me, too.

———

Although it was difficult to understand all that was happening to me, I was surprised that I was not tired. Considering the tremendous distances I had already traveled, generally I would have been exhausted. My family and friends near me understood my bewilderment, and it delighted them. The atmosphere in the party was electric— there was music, dancing, and amazing food.

So much celebration, yet the central focus was just the fellowship and being able to see these people from my life all over again. They welcomed me to Heaven. What do you say to that? I replied, "Thank you!"

You know, Jimmy, how we react on Earth upon arriving somewhere new: What will I be doing? Where will I be staying? When do I need to be there? My hosts told me that my new body would need no sleep, yet there would be plenty of opportunities for rest. I have to say, the last thing I wanted to do now was rest.

Looking around, I recognized teachers and classmates, relatives and friends, neighbors and acquaintances... so many were there for this amazing reunion to celebrate my return. Loved ones and acquaintances I had known from all of my years on Earth now surrounded me. I saw my aunts and uncles, and I saw my grandparents.

———

Ecstatically, I shook hands with everyone, and that alone must have taken an eternity. Just being around all of those familiar faces again was exhilarating. Everyone was young, and so happy—happier than I had seen them on Earth.

The Lord has told us the truth, Jimmy... He is the God of the Living, not the God of the dead (Mark 12:27).

Everything seemed alive, including our surroundings. Let me explain the interior design of this Lodge.

God the Almighty Father sits high upon His throne, and rejoices in all of His Creation (Psalm 104:31). He loves a good view. No matter where one stands, or which home one find himself in, there is an amazing view. This hall was no different. The first floor, which I had just entered, was about the size of the interior of any large country clubhouse. Looking out through the windows, you saw an incredible view.

The golf course was below, but there were immense waterfalls, meadows, and incredible drops throughout the course and the surrounding terrain. The hills and valleys in the distance provided a perfect backdrop.

Off to the right of the golf course was a huge lake, a blue shimmering lake that reflected the clouds in the sky. Far off, there was a marina in a cove complete with anchored boats to take on the lake. Beaches and forests surrounded the water's edges. The lake seemed alive—waving in rhythm with the clouds and the breeze, with a bed of glistening crystals clearly visible on the bottom.

Just on the outside of these windows was an open deck. People were sitting in chairs, talking, laughing and enjoying the view. Back inside the front room, one could *think* the word "glass," and the glass walls would stay. To let the breeze in and hear the sounds of the outside birds, a simple thought, "remove glass," would make the glass immediately vanish.

The interior of this room was warm and earthy; polished but comfortable. The workmanship on the walls and ceilings captured my attention. My old pets walked around. Do you remember Kelly, our old beagle? She was healthy and happy again.

Nancy and my parents stood next to me while I looked around the room admiring the place. Then, they directed my attention to the wall behind me.

While a bar or restaurant on Earth might have pictures or televisions hanging on the walls, here there were similar large "screens" that the people were all watching. The rectangular screens were now showing scenes from my life, Jimmy, everyone was watching *my* earthly life.

These were more than just old videos. My friends and family all gathered around watching the scenes, experiencing the moments as if in real time. The scenes revisited the times when the Lord was most pleased with my life. Each moment was featured as a specific time in which I had lived as a true follower of Christ.

I watched one of the frames. Do you remember the Korean boy that came to live with us in the 1950s, Jimmy? I had heard from someone at church that there was a foreign exchange student who had come to the U.S. and needed a home. Because I had learned a little Korean when I was overseas, I thought it would be a perfect opportunity to invite the young man to stay with us. And it went fine for a bit. However, the young man breached my trust, and stole some of our belongings. At the time, it angered me that we had opened our home to this young person but he had not followed our rules.

I watched the scene of this kid playing outside with you guys, and the boy was laughing along with you. I had not thought about him in years, and I certainly didn't expect to see this chapter from my life playing in front of me now. Not only were the audio and visual details of the moments exposed, but also the emotions of everyone involved. Every thought and every feeling of each person on the screen was perceptible as if we witnessed the event through God's very own eyes.

As we watched, text accompanied the replays. Beneath the scene of the boy playing with you and your siblings were the words, "I was a stranger and you invited me in. - Matthew 25:35." It didn't matter now that the young man had ended up stealing from us. What mattered was that I had shown him love. Everything else was between the young man and the Lord.

All across this big banquet hall was a sort of highlight reel playing on the screens, showing other moments from my life when I had most honored God. On Earth, I would have been embarrassed by this kind of attention; here, however, it all felt more like a wedding in its celebratory mood. My parents stood there with beaming smiles, showing their pride.

Then, I looked at Nancy, who was also smiling. I told her these videos shed a slightly more favorable light on my life than what may have actually happened. I jokingly asked her what they did with all the other videos from my life. She laughed, and said I would have to take that up with the Lord when I saw Him. "He picks out all of the moments that are shown up here, personally," she added.

Then Nancy quoted Psalm 103:12, "Remember Jim, 'As far as the east is from the west, So far has He removed our transgressions from us.'"

Thanks to Christ, videos of my worst moments no longer existed, and those moments had been erased from my record forever.

———

We all continued to talk and laugh, and I ate some of the food. I know what you are thinking right now, Jimmy. Because I'd be thinking it, too.

Yes, there is beer here…and it is phenomenal. There is also wine here, and of course, it's the best. But the drinks up here are different. They are delicious and refreshing. Remember that alcohol is formed on Earth resulting from a fermentation process. In Heaven, there is no death, nor rotting, nor decay. Our beer does not contain alcohol.

We call it Light beer.

— 10 —
HALLOWED HALLS

As I walked around, mingling and drinking, a structure caught my attention in the room. At the far end of the Lodge, an incredible spiral staircase started in the level below, rose up through the main room, through the ceiling and into the story above. The twisting rails were made of the same ancient, amber colored wood as the front doors. The steps, however, were what really captivated me.

Stone steps, made of an iridescent and liquid-like composite, glowed and refracted the light while turning themselves up and around the spiral casing. The staircase was like some kind of floating escalator. I looked down at the level underneath, just to see how the moving parts returned along their path. Looking at each step was like looking at a stained glass window, and the material absorbed and reflected the light that was pouring into the room.

I stared at the design of the staircase, transfixed. I just kept staring at these stairs. Then, when I finally looked away, everyone was now staring at me.

Their thoughts and their excitement actually entered my thoughts—they were imploring me to step on the stairwell and go up. The guests raised their glasses and gave a loud cheer.

Looking at the opening in the ceiling high above me and then looking back at my family and friends, I waved, stepped upon one of the glowing stones, and slowly rose into the upper level.

———

I found myself ascending about twenty feet up through the wide oculus. The ceiling of the first floor, through which I was now passing, was crafted with a rich coffered paneling. I looked through the opening as I entered a brand new space. The step came to a stop, and I walked off the stairwell and into what I can best describe as a hallowed and decorated museum.

A large and vaulted room surrounded me like the airy and magnificent atmosphere of some great library. Beams of light streamed in from the windows high above. Murals covered the ceiling; many I recognized as scenes from times in my World War II days.

Looking around the awe-inspiring space, I tried to take in all I was seeing. There were displays and models—an amazing array of memorials, yet everything was arranged so that all could not be seen at once. Clearly, this space was for exploring and experiencing in a myriad of different ways.

My eyes continued to search the whole expanse, and finally my focus came to the exhibit right in front of me: a single black cannon. It was shining as if it had just arrived straight from some factory. I walked up to it, and read the inscription:

THE MORNING CANNON

DURING THE BOMBARDMENT OF FT. McHENRY,

MARYLAND

FIRED BY THE UNITED STATES COMPANY

of SEA FENCIBLES

SEPT. 13-14, 1814

WHEN BY THE LIGHT OF "BOMBS BURSTING IN AIR"

THE NATIONAL ANTHEM - THE STAR SPANGLED

BANNER HAD ITS BIRTH

"Hello, Jim," I heard a voice say as I turned from the cannon. Standing in front of me was a young man, about 25 or 30 years old. "I'm George McNeir," he said, "I'm your great-great-great grandfather."

———

It's funny, Jimmy. Can you imagine meeting someone you had never met, knowing instantly that you are related from generations ago? I looked at this man and recognized some of his features from the family I had known on Earth.

I must have appeared to him as a young man, as well. We were polite to each other, as new acquaintances, yet it also felt like I knew him well enough to talk casually. I began asking him questions like I might ask a longtime friend. Thus, we began to speak more comfortably, and I asked him why I was standing in this impressive museum.

"It's something, isn't it?" he said. "Because you are welcome here, the Lord has taken our service to others very seriously," he said. "You descend from a long line of individuals who defended both country and family. As a gift, the Lord built this museum to commemorate our mutual services on Earth."

Continuing, he explained, "Christ interacted with soldiers while He lived on Earth, and He treated them with great dignity. The Lord values service, and honors our sacrifice. However, we were not to try and attain our treasures on Earth, 'where moth and rust destroy' (Matthew 6:19). Instead, the Father has preserved the proof of our sacrifices here in Heaven, where they will be remembered forever."

Surely I must have appeared dumbfounded as I surveyed the decorated walls and ceilings, so he continued, "Let me tell you about my life, Jim."

———

"In the year 1812, I was 36 years old. I was a self-employed tailor in Baltimore, and I had a wife and four children at home.

"Baltimore, like many port towns along the East Coast in those days, was a city in turmoil. What you know as the War of 1812 had begun, affecting everyone's daily life. The British Royal Navy appeared in harbors up and down the Eastern seaboard, and trade came to a halt.

"I loved my family very much and I provided for them. We lived in a nice home, if not a bit crowded. The main goods I manufactured and sold were Great Coats, and I sent many of my coats to customers in Europe who found it fashionable to have a jacket made in the New World.

"I worked out of my house near South Calvert Street and Market. It was a good life being able to wake up with my family, and make a product for a living.

"My father's generation had secured our freedom from the British years before in the Revolutionary War. But the citizens of Maryland, and the other colonies, never felt we had been granted our rightful independence from Great Britain. In fact, Mr. Charles Carroll, the oldest signer of the Declaration of Independence, lived not far from my home. Even in his advanced age he was a constant presence in the town, strolling along the shops in the morning. The local people respected him. As the British embargoes began, we would secretly convene in our neighbors' homes, helping each other as the enemy sought to break our will.

"During the daylight hours, we tried to carry on as best as possible. Exports were blocked by the British and trade slowed. Eventually, I went broke and could not pay my rent. To keep from losing our house, I had to sell my remaining inventory; by April 1813, the bank had seized the rest of my assets.

"Jim, I looked at my young family, and I prayed to our Heavenly Father. It was now late 1813, and the months that followed were difficult. Finally, I volunteered to serve with the Sea Fencibles, stationed at Fort McHenry, just outside the city. The military didn't pay much, but every penny helped provide for my family.

"March 22, 1814, I was appointed third Lieutenant. By now, the war was going badly for our country and it wasn't just our families' livelihoods for which we now fought. Our young nation was under attack. The newspapers were filled with fearful accounts of the atrocities and abuses under the command of British captain, William Smith.

"Enemy troops landed in Washington D.C. August 1814, and both The White House and The Capitol were burned and destroyed later that month. At Fort McHenry, I was put in command of the cannoneers on the water battery. It was our job to make sure those boats were repelled if they ever showed up in Baltimore, now that they had already laid siege to our nation's capital."

George paused for a moment and continued, "I have to say, Jim, that I watched your life very closely. I cheered your courage as you left to fight in wars far away from your loved ones, and as you traveled to foreign countries to protect freedoms for other nations. Yet, my neighbors and I were forced to take up arms just minutes away from our own homes. With an enemy as formidable as the British Royal Navy on the horizon, it was a fearful time for us all.

"Sure enough, those British boats showed up in our harbor on September 12, 1814. Even though I had been drilling the men on cannons for many months, we were no match for the long guns of the Royal Navy. From their ships, they could launch a 200-pound ball the distance of two nautical miles, and we knew we were vulnerable.

"I had not been able to leave the Fort in weeks. My family sustained themselves on my meager salary, and I stayed in correspondence with my wife through the mail so as not to abandon my post. The only thing standing between those enemy ships and my home was our local group of volunteers.

"We all knew we had to rely on God."

———

"When the first British shells crashed into Fort McHenry, one could hear the concussions all the way through the streets of Baltimore. Pinned down behind the battery bulwarks, we awaited orders from command. Our cannons had no chance of reaching the British ships positioned that far away, and so the officer of the Fort instructed us to cease fire.

"For twenty-five hours, those ships bombarded us with the most ammunition unloaded on any single target during the entire war. Throughout the day and night of

September 13, what could we do? We stayed low and we prayed.

"As the night wore on, the bombardment continued unceasingly. Finally, the explosions subsided; and when morning broke, a strange silence filled the air as the British contemplated their next move.

"We had survived. The men rallied, and the little, torn flag that had somehow survived the night was retrieved from its post. Then, the commanding officer ordered the hand-stitched flag that had just been given to the garrison fetched, and the colors run high. A lawyer present at the Fort, Francis Scott Key, was negotiating the release of a prisoner and watched the flag being raised.

"What a site to behold, Jim. The boys all cheered, and I told the men to fire off a couple rounds just to let those Brits know we were still alive. Although the warships had bombed our Fort to bits, they eventually turned their lightened loads around and left the city of Baltimore for good.

"Our city and families, including my own, were safe. In retrospect, is it any wonder why the good Lord blessed our great country with the famous National Anthem that commemorates our determinedness on that very specific day and night?"

Looking up, I saw in the center of the ceiling, the words inscribed in a massive mural surrounded by the images of angels:

O say can you see, by the dawn's early light,
What so proudly we hailed at the twilight's last gleaming,
Whose broad stripes and bright stars through the perilous fight,
O'er the ramparts we watched, were so gallantly streaming?
And the rockets' red glare, the bombs bursting in air,
Gave proof through the night that our flag was still there;
O say does that star-spangled banner yet wave
O'er the land of the free and the home of the brave?

On the shore dimly seen through the mists of the deep,
Where the foe's haughty host in dread silence reposes,
What is that which the breeze, o'er the towering steep,
As it fitfully blows, half conceals, half discloses?
Now it catches the gleam of the morning's first beam,
In full glory reflected now shines in the stream:
'Tis the star-spangled banner, O long may it wave
O'er the land of the free and the home of the brave.

And where is that band who so vauntingly swore
That the havoc of war and the battle's confusion,

A home and a country, should leave us no more?
Their blood has washed out their foul footsteps' pollution.
No refuge could save the hireling and slave
From the terror of flight, or the gloom of the grave:
And the star-spangled banner in triumph doth wave,
O'er the land of the free and the home of the brave.

O thus be it ever, when freemen shall stand
Between their loved homes and the war's desolation.
Blest with vict'ry and peace, may the Heav'n rescued land
Praise the Power that hath made and preserved us a nation!
Then conquer we must, when our cause it is just,
And this be our motto: 'In God is our trust.'
And the star-spangled banner in triumph shall wave
O'er the land of the free and the home of the brave!

Grandfather George and I talked a little more as we walked down the middle of the hall, enjoying both the paintings and the displays. Everything seemed so perfectly ordered. What a curator of important moments our God is, Jimmy. "How great are his signs, how mighty his wonders! His kingdom is an eternal kingdom; his dominion endures from generation to generation" (Daniel 4:3). Impressed with the magnitude of this fore-father of mine, I respectfully reached out to shake his hand, and said what a thrill it was to meet him, to have him as my relative, and to share in these mighty wonders—commemorating generation to generation.

———

Now we stood in front of a small marble island. There was a partition, a bit of a wall sectioning us off from the rest of the corridor. I couldn't help but notice this small display. On the little island were several peculiar, interesting objects.

I saw a bucket of water, with ice floating in it. Next to the bucket was a wooden board, about four feet long and one foot wide. Strewn around the bucket and board were beautiful flowers, vivid and colorful, still connected to their stems.

Another man walked up to the marble island.

"Jim," said George. "This is my grandson, Michael McEnnis… your great-grandfather."

— 11 —
MICHAEL McENNIS

I know what you're thinking, Jimmy, but stick with me. We're not just a bunch of old dead guys up here.

I took one look at this man who walked up to me, and I thought I was looking at all three of my sons at the same time... even seeing characteristics of my own grandchildren in his face.

Generations matter to the Lord, Jimmy. Christ has the same eyes as His ancestor, King David. They are the eyes that didn't flinch at Goliath on the battlefield, and they didn't flinch when Pilate sentenced Him to death, either.

Obviously, Grandfather Michael McEnnis and I share a few of the same features, too. Shaking hands with him, I told him that Grandfather George had just reviewed his earthly life in Baltimore for me.

Michael replied, "I was born in Baltimore, and lived there until my father, John McEnnis, moved to St. Louis in 1837. The rest of our family soon followed."

"When I was eleven years old, I traveled by stagecoach from Baltimore to St. Louis with my mother and my younger siblings. It was a cold trip in the winter, and my mother struggled to keep her younger children calm as we traveled across the icy rivers and frozen passes. Before he left, my father had already gone ahead, and told me I would now be the protector of the family on our journey."

I found his story captivating, but, in the back of my mind I was still wondering about the arrangement of the bucket of water, flowers, and the wooden board in front of me. Michael continued his story.

"When I was twenty-one years old, James Polk declared war on Mexico. There was a dispute between our two countries over the boundaries of the United States. A call for volunteers went out, and I signed up in the Army's Muster Role for a twelve month tour, starting in the spring of 1846. Our orders were to take a riverboat from St. Louis to Fort Leavenworth. From there, we would be marching all the way from Kansas City to Santa Fe; walking through the Kansas territories, Colorado, and on to New Mexico.

"May 14, 1846 was a beautiful day in St. Louis. The sun was shining brightly and we had all gathered on Twelfth Street. In line formation, we marched east on Pine Street to the levee where we boarded the steamer, *Pride of the West*. Our horses were put on the lower deck, while we climbed to the upper level where we waved goodbye to the women standing on the levee. As the boat backed out, we fired the cannon from the bow to the cheers of the onlookers.

"Several weeks later, the *Pride of the West* arrived at Fort Leavenworth, Kansas. There, we left the river and we began our march through the prairie, because at that time there were no railroads past Kansas City. The weather was hot, and many men suffered on that long summer journey, walking over the Great Plains.

"All along that burning march I recalled the long, cold trip I had made as a boy from Maryland to Missouri. Now, I was traveling west across the rest of the continent, battling the extreme heat instead of the icy cold.

"We struggled through the Rockies, climbing over mountains so steep that the horses could not haul the wagons and heavy cannon. We had to drag the cargo over the canyons with long ropes. Then, after we had made it through the mountain passes, General Kearny marched us hard as we trudged over the burning and parched desert.

"But Jim, I loved it. It was difficult, but exhilarating. The West was an incredible site to behold... a landscape with a spirit about it. Twenty-two members of our family had fought in the American Revolution, and forty-eight members, like George, had fought in the War of 1812. This was *my* chance to answer my country's call.

"When our company finally reached Santa Fe in November 1846, Dr. George Penn, of Arrow Rock, Missouri, was sent back to Fort Leavenworth with dispatches. I was one of five soldiers selected by the General to accompany Penn back as a bodyguard.

"I had finally arrived at the warfront in New Mexico, only to be ordered right back to the Fort in Kansas. Because it was late fall, the ground was covered with snow and it was now very cold. There were only sixteen of us, and as we headed back through the Kansas territory, we were attacked by a group of Navajo warriors.

"Being extremely afraid, I instinctively ran at the group with my sword drawn, charging and yelling at the top of my lungs. I had heard that the Navajo fought like wolves —chasing their prey on the run, yet sometimes running away when chased. Luckily for us, the warriors retreated; and my fellow soldiers told me that it was because of me leading the way that they also joined in the fight.

"I told the men that at least on the prairie, the bigger the coward, the harder he'll fight! No one wanted to fall prey to a war party alone on the frontier. The rest of the return went fine, and eventually we made it safely back to Fort Leavenworth with our correspondences."

———

Michael continued, "It was now early 1847 at Fort Leavenworth. I assumed my orders would be to return to the West when spring arrived, and rejoin our dragoon that was now in California.

"However, a letter from St. Louis reached me at the Fort, telling me that my father had suddenly become ill and died. I was crushed by the news. When I had left St. Louis, my father was in good health. Adding to my grief was the knowledge that my mother and younger siblings were now left all alone in St. Louis, fending for themselves.

"Showing the letter to my commanding officer at Fort Leavenworth, I was granted leave to return home, at once. As I traveled back, I remembered what my father had once told me as a child, before we set out on that cold journey from Baltimore. He told me it would be my responsibility to watch over the family in his absence."

———

Listening to Michael, I nodded. He left the military to attend to his family back home. He paused next to the table of objects, and continued his story.

"Returning home to my family, overwhelmed me. Obviously, I needed to support our family; thankfully, I found employment as a clerk for Chouteau & Valle, a large wholesale grocer and commission house on Front Street downtown.

"In addition to working as a brewer, my father had also been the superintendent of the old Catholic Graveyard on Franklin and Jefferson Avenues. After he died in 1847, the Archbishop appointed my mother as superintendent, and my brother took charge of the graveyard responsibilities at the age of sixteen, along with another friend. The two boys knew almost every grave and had done a good job managing the increasing burials and demands on the property.

"Then, in 1849, St. Louis experienced a cholera epidemic and many were dying.

"Because of the conditions in the graveyard, my brother grew sick and had to be carried home on a litter. Four of his men had died, too. The graveyard was unattended, with corpses piling up, including eight bodies lying in the graveyard with no one to bury them, nor attend to their remains. With my younger brother sick, I was told that I must come assist at once, and take charge of the cemetery.

"My friends and employers all protested, not only on account of the danger, but because they thought I was physically unfit to do the work all by myself. With the help of two friends working all day and into the night, we kept the place clear, but the number of the dead filled up the graveyard so fast that there were few burial plots.

"I asked the Archbishop for permission to start another cemetery to accommodate the number of victims from the ravaging disease. Thus, he established Rock Springs Cemetery, located deep in the woods with not even a fence around the perimeter.

"I dug the first grave. Besides the sick and the dying, the population of St. Louis also plummeted because so many left to avoid a similar plight. Whole blocks of houses were empty, and many dwellings were abandoned with the homeowners leaving their goods behind them. Because of the cholera, it was impossible to get laborers as there was a scarcity of young men and fear swept the community. However, I was able to employ the help of some teenagers for an average of four dollars a day, who worked hard and were very brave—the difficult work and the damp, foul atmosphere threatened us daily.

"Because so many had died or been hospitalized, the public became so poor they could hardly buy food or bury their dead, and the Archbishop issued free graves and labor to all who were unable to pay. The scenes of sorrow, grief and distress of that year remained with me all my life.

"On a very hot day, near the end of the cholera outbreak, I was standing at the graveyard gate. Coming up the road was a woman carrying a large bundle… I stepped out, seeing that she was staggering under the load, and invited her to come into the shade of a tree and rest.

"She walked in, placed the bundle on the grass and laid down beside it, exhausted. I ran and brought her a bucket of ice water, which appeared to revive her slightly, so I walked away, keeping my eye on her.

"After some time she arose, and I went over to tell her to stay longer, but her answer was that she had to get back to town. She then handed me a 'poor ticket,' for the grave of a child of twelve years old; Feeling that was fine, I asked when the remains would be brought.

"The woman answered, pointing to her bundle, 'She is here.' Then, she told me her husband and one child had previously died from cholera, now this child was the last. She did not have one cent for a grave, so she had gone to the Archbishop for a free plot. After meeting with him at the church, she went home, wrapped her darling in a quilt and carried her in her arms to the graveyard.

"Her story broke my heart. Telling her to sit down, I asked her to wait while a grave was prepared. Then, I got some boards and made a box for the remains. I laid flowers all around the body, lowered the box into a grave, covered the tops with leaves, so as to prevent the sound of the earth over the box, filled in the earth, and placed a board at the head of the grave.

"After we had paid our respects, I walked with the poor mother to the gate. Turning around, she told me she was the last of her people and very likely I would bury her remains the following week. With tears in here eyes, she held out her hand and thanked me for the comfort I had given her, and walked away."

A silence surrounded Michael and me.

Then, he looked at me intently and said, "Here in Heaven, blessed are the poor in spirit. For this Kingdom of God is truly theirs. That mother is now reunited with her child and family, and all are happy again. God remembered her loss and her poor family's suffering. That is also why He has commemorated my own service, not with a sword or a rifle, but with these simple gifts given to a poor woman, who had lost her dear child."

I looked at the water, and the flowers, and the wooden plank once used as a grave marker. Michael and George had not told me their stories to brag, but rather that I might better understand God's goodness here in our new home.

We shared a few more words, and then my two grandfathers walked away, leaving me alone to contemplate other displays. It was amazing to meet these family members from our shared heritage, Jimmy. Yet, the museum housed even more treasures… still to be discovered.

— 12 —

The UNKNOWN PILOT

Stepping away from the humble display, I walked out into an open area, and suddenly it was as if the entire museum reacted to my desire to see what was next.

The lighting changed, the mood shifted, and the room transformed into the very walls of that old Carpenter's Soda Shop where I had played pinball at the age of eighteen.

Music filled the air from the 1940s. A radio voice crackled, "This is no joke; this is an act of war!" as the announcer described the attack on Pearl Harbor all over again. It felt like so long ago, but I remembered every detail. Looking around, I waited to see myself, or some of my old friends again... anyone in this familiar setting. The lighting was dim and dramatic, and I focused on what was in front of me.

The wall forming the back of the room was like a curtain, and caught my attention as it swayed. Sounds of the soda pop joint faded into the background.

Suddenly, the curtain split and slowly opened. No longer was the setting around me that of the dingy old drug store. As if on a conveyer belt, I was brought through the parting curtains and into the wide expanse of a shining airplane hanger. In front of me now in this brightly illuminated display room, was a sight I thought I'd never see again. She was big, she was beautiful, and she was a bomber's best friend. She was the *Lil' Pecker*.

What a moment. There was my old plane, but she looked brand new again. The *Lil' Pecker* was right in front of me, out in the middle of the open atrium. She was sparkling with a fresh coat of paint, and a mirror image of the shiny metal body reflected off the marble floor.

My eyes went immediately to the cockpit. Yes, my tally marks for every one of my ninety-eight missions were still there, right under the port side of the windshield.

The plane was a deep olive color with her trademarked cylindrical white nose. Sitting back on her haunches with her prop held high, she looked like a bulldog ready to bite. They nicknamed a plane like her "The Jug" because of the wide set landing gear and tank-like fuselage. She was actually just a few feet wider than she was long.

Her four prop blades, each one taller than a man, were elevated above my head—just waiting to rip through the sky. Painted yellow tips accentuated the "X" shape of the props that protruded from her flat nose. The machine guns were polished, and the wings stretched wide across the hall.

There on the front was that signature woodpecker... smiling his big red-headed grin; with yellow feet and a bright, blue butt.

I walked towards the plane and put my hand on her side. Looking down at the shiny black tires, the red and white pinwheels painted inside the rotors brought back memories—working alongside the mechanics underneath the aircraft, down near the landing gear.

Ducking down, I walked below the nose and looked under the plane. Sure enough, just as if I were back on the airfield, I saw two legs sticking out from beneath the plane's belly.

———

On a cart came rolling out from underneath a man who stood up and gave me a hug. I had never seen this stranger before. He wore a khaki flight suit with his sleeves rolled up and belt cinched high around his waist.

Grinning widely, he asked, "Well, what do ya, think?"

"Amazing. Better than I ever remember her," I replied.

"Originally designed by Mr. Alexander Kartveli, with a Pratt & Whitney R2800, turbo-supercharged, 18 cylinder air cooled radial engine, rated at over 2,000 horsepower. One of

15,683 ever made. I've been working on her for a while. Just waiting for today, Jim."

I looked at him, again, intently, and still did not recognize him.

"I love planes," he said, "and when the Lord asked me to put the finishing touches on the *Lil' Pecker*, it was a dream come true."

———

I stared at him, confused.

"You don't know me, Jim, but I know you. Every time you flew, and I mean every time you flew, I would head to one of the observation rooms and watch what was happening down on the Earth.

"The Good Book says, 'We are surrounded by such a great cloud of witnesses' (Hebrews 12:1), and let's just say I was there in the clouds, witnessing it all right there alongside you.

"Do you remember early January, 1944, Jim? You were returning to England from a combat mission over France after one of your wheels had been shot out from under you. As you were approaching the runway, you knew you'd be making an emergency landing—likely resulting in a forced spinout. The trick was to hold the stick back with as much strength as you could muster until the speed slowed, causing the aircraft to pitch forward and spin on its wing to a stop. If you didn't time it right, the Thunderbolt would be going too fast, would flip, and explode.

"You pulled it out, though, and made a textbook two-point landing, Jim. Most of it was just great piloting... *most* of it," he said with a wink.

"You see, I wanted to be a fighter pilot myself. In fact, I was was well on my way, and by the summer of 1942 my log book showed that I was right where I needed to be.

"But on September 17, it was foggy on the Randolph Field airstrip. I was scheduled to make my solo flight, so I took off and reached cruising altitude. I completed my maneuvers, despite visibility being so bad.

"The next thing I heard over my headset was someone calling my aircraft number, ordering me back to the runway. You remember how many planes we'd have up in the sky during those training runs? Well, on that day, the flight control couldn't see who was who. I guess they got confused. I didn't know where I was supposed to be, listening to those air traffic controllers.

"By now you know the rest. I saw the strip below, and I came in hard when I thought they had given me clearance. I had been turned around and was now approaching from the north. I dropped below the clouds, and as soon as there was visibility, I saw the blur of your plane.

"And then I saw a bright, white flash. The next thing I knew, I was up here."

———

I looked at the young man's face and then at his body. This was the other pilot who had died in my accident, back in 1942. Shocked, I didn't know what to say.

"I'm sorry that you did not make it," I finally said.

He smiled and replied, "Oh, it's okay, it was all in God's plan for both of us. Not only did I end up here, but you got a better looking nose after all those surgeries," he said.

"And you became a great pilot," he added.

The man invited me to step up and sit in the cockpit, just like I had done so many years before. Walking along the wing and then crawling in through the canopy, I sat down in the seat, and looked at all the sparkling instruments. I remembered that the cockpit of the Thunderbolt was roomier than the newer fighters; The Jug's interior wasn't as ergonomic as the modern jets. Now, everything glistened. Gone was the stale smell of vomit and oil that would always greet me during my departures, a residual effect from the many others who had flown the aircraft. That odor was gone —replaced by a clean, metallic scent.

I knew this plane could fly. All it was waiting for was the command from its pilot.

"You were shot down in Korea and you hadn't flown long enough with the 67th to even name your own plane," my new friend said. "But there are plenty of guys from your old squadron up here. I talked to several of them and they'd love to have you fly any of their Mustangs. And if you want one of your own, well, all you have to do is just ask. There's plenty of room in the hangar. And we've got lots of air shows up here!" he exclaimed, throwing his arms out wide.

———

Walking around the hall talking about planes with this young man, I realized something. God cares about our hobbies and He cares about our interests. Our lives are more exciting when we get to experience passion. Yet, we often can't dedicate our entire earthly lives to our hobbies and interests. We have to labor; we have to work and sustain ourselves. On Earth, we live to exist… in Heaven, we exist to live.

We get to expand upon our God-given gifts up here, and perfect our talents. If one loves creating, one can paint or sculpt, and if one loves being technical, one can engineer or invent new devices. If someone loves to be hospitable, he or she hosts big events. In Heaven, the Lord blesses us with ways to utilize our talents and our passions.

I talked to this pilot for a long time, and I learned about his life and his own family. Shaking my new friend's hand and thanking him for his work, I told him I couldn't wait to fly the plane again.

Yet, I wanted to keep going. There were many other alcoves and hallways leading to more exhibits, relics and displays. As I walked behind the plane, admiring my old call numbers painted on the tail, something further down the hall caught my eye. Music emanated from a hallway off in the distance. I looked towards the direction of the sound, and saw colored lights reflecting off the floor from a room far away... beckoning me closer.

— 13 —
The JUKEBOX

The music became softer the closer I came. I turned a corner, and there, in front of a brightly lit wall, was a jukebox.

It was big... probably ten feet tall, pulsating with light as neon oils rushed through its tubular contours. The jukebox was captivating—glowing as if the Holy Spirit Himself was electrifying it—buzzing and supercharged by some kind of heavenly voltage. Streaks of light swirled and popped around its edges, and millions of songs were somehow displayed in its queue all at once.

Yet this playlist was customized for one person, in particular. There was a golden plaque on the wall next to the machine inscribed:

Alone in Vietnam,
As night was drawing near,
He wrote down a list of songs
To keep away the fear.

'If I return alive,'

The man said to himself,
'I'll buy a hundred records
And keep them on a shelf.'

Writing songs in order,
With shaky hand and pen,
He lost the list soon after,
When rockets came again.

Jimmy, this jukebox had all of your songs, ready to play on this incredible device. It contained all your favorites from when you were young: songs from the fifties and songs from the sixties. Everything from that old list that you wrote down in the jungle in 1968 was now ready to burst forth in sound. I knew there were countless other songs that could be called up in an instant, just by thought. But only by *your* thought.

It suddenly occurred to me, Jimmy. You were always the happiest when you had your music playing, in the car, on family gatherings and trips. Why had I not realized that earlier? Music made you happy! Of course, the Lord knew. He had always known you best, and here He had built this jukebox: customized for you.

He felt your pain when you served, and He remembered you in the trenches—He knew your fears and sufferings!

There is a new place being built here, Jimmy, a Diner. This Diner is not far from my Lodge here in Heaven, and it is almost finished. It will be a place where your friends and family will go, where we can will listen to this jukebox together, and you can choose the songs. All you have to do is get here... and, when the Diner is finished, the sign will flash in neon lights, *Jimmy's Jukebox*.

We will watch sports together again there, Jimmy. We will laugh and we will drink together. We will listen to music, and there will be live acts, and food, and dancing. It is all here, Jimmy, and He has made that place just for you. I get the museum and the golf course. You get the diner. And we get to share it all in fellowship, in family... and in the victory that is in Christ Jesus.

— 14 —

St. ROSE *of* HEAVEN

Seeing that jukebox, my heart felt like it might explode all over again. But, there are no tears up here, Jimmy, as He has wiped them all away. Instead, my heart was bursting with happiness, as I began to understand just how much God loves my son.

At that moment, I knew that God has a special place for you; He has a special place for your brothers and your sister; and He has a special place for your mother. I was experiencing the special eternity that He had created for me.

I walked back down to the main level below the museum and exited through the large bay doors at the far end of the Lodge. Walking along the same gemstone path, I continued through a beautiful garden, but was still thinking about what I had just seen.

One object, a cannon: a weapon of war that won us the song of freedom and our National Anthem; another object, a jukebox: a joyful reward for my son's faithfulness to our country. Yet, there were empty rooms I had seen in the museum, still to be filled by future acts of service.

122

Now my surroundings caught my attention because the aroma around me was intoxicating. Cultivated roses as big as softballs were blooming in this garden. Looking ahead through the woods, I saw a beautiful church standing in a clearing halfway up a hill. As I approached, I could see it glowing as if it were alive. Ornately engraved upon the church façade were these words, "St. Rose of Heaven."

———

The smell was so sweet and intense that I felt I was surrounded by holiness. The Lord was close now; I knew it. I quickly walked towards that church, eager to go inside.

Amazingly, the sky in Heaven changes somewhat like our earthly sky. As I walked, a deep pink heavenly hue now set off the cool tones of the stone church. The building shone as if the old limestone structure had now been masoned out of pure diamonds. This was our old church, yet it was all made new again. It was as if my journey had come to an end… or perhaps it was just beginning.

On Earth, St. Rose of Lima sat on Maple Street. Your mother and I were married there on November 18, 1944. She was Mary Rose Wientge, and for much of her life she went by Mary Rose.

This is where I had worn my dress uniform and waited for your mother at the altar. I remembered those moments as I reached out my hand… clutching the familiar handle of the church's entrance.

Once more, I gazed up at the façade, before I entered. The steeple penetrated the sky like a spire signaling God's strength. Standing there again on that threshold made me think of your mother, and of that happy wedding day. I remembered how much I loved her in her youth, and how I loved her even more later in life, and how she, just like this very church, had sustained me throughout the many seasons of my earthly life.

This time, there was no ailing heart holding me back. The church's pillars were tall, palatial, and inviting—no longer preventing me from coming closer. I was finally entering God's own home.

I walked in, and there He sat in a pew, up towards the front and on the right. The nave and apse of the church were on fire with His radiance; He illuminated the entire space. His left hand was resting on the back of the wooden bench, and I saw the deep mark. My heart was beating a thousand miles an hour. I walked up the aisle, up to His front row, right into the pew… and I forgot to genuflect.

———

Automatically my hand moved over my heart; I felt like I had nearly lost my ability to speak. I could see a million years all at once in His eyes. Every man and woman that He had created were visible in an instant in His eyes, and I could feel the love that He had for each of them. At the same time, it seemed at that moment as if I were the only human being in the universe that mattered to Him.

He was smiling. Actually, He was beaming. While I had hugged a lot of people back on Earth, and quite a few up here in Heaven, no hug compared to this embrace. After all I had been through in my life, it was time to finally meet my Maker. I sat with the Lord, and we talked. Whether it was twenty minutes or twenty years, I do not know; time is of no importance here.

I wanted to know if it was really God that I had encountered when I had flatlined in that recovery room in 1982. Jesus laughed and asked me who else I thought it could have been. Although the enemy can disguise himself as an angel of light (2 Cor. 11:14), it is only the Father who grants us free will, according to Christ. After all, God had asked me if I wanted to come home to Heaven, or return to Earth.

Those twelve extra years I was given with my family were His gift.

Curious if what I was taught about Christ was true, I asked Him about His own life, and He showed me actual scenes; replayed right in front of us on the altar. I was familiar with many of the moments and stories, others were new to me.

Amazingly, I asked Him what things were in store for you and your siblings, Jimmy. What great plans He had for your children, and their children. I even asked Him how many generations would continue and what would happen in the future on Earth. He replied that, "in all things God works for the good of those who love him, who have been called according to his purpose" (Romans 8:28).

Christ reminded me that everything in Heaven moves on the Father's schedule, and from what I can tell up here, God really doesn't like to rush things.

Jimmy, when you and I grew up, religion was taught as a discipline. Just as schoolwork exercised our minds, and athletics exercised our bodies, often times religion was taught to keep us on the "straight and narrow." That discipline served us well in the military... at least it did if you said as many memorized prayers as I did when the bullets were flying all around.

Yet when the subject of the afterlife came up, we were taught that Heaven was some sort of far-off existence, rather than a real, physical place. Perhaps our religion teachers even struggled to imagine Heaven, themselves. Those vague descriptions never resonated with my young imagination.

Why would I care about a realm devoid of the things I liked and enjoyed? As a boy, I was interested in playgrounds, candy, pets, and baseball. In comparison, the heaven of harps and never-ending church services sounded boring to me.

However, here I was finding out that version of Heaven was untrue.

God created us human, and he wants us to live happily as humans. He is the God of the living (Mark 12:27). He made us in His image (Gen. 1:27). Only by sharing in His death can we break free from the chains of sin on Earth, just as we were before "the fall."

After the Resurrection, nothing contained Christ— neither walls, nor time, nor distance. He even appeared to His disciples simultaneously; miles away from each other at the same time. He entered locked rooms, He disguised his features, played tricks on his friends, and He loved every minute of it.

Jimmy, if time and space can no longer contain our glorified heavenly bodies, can you imagine the feeling of being freed from your current physical pains?

He died for us, so that you don't have to fear anymore, Jimmy. You will feel the sunshine on your neck and hear the birds chirp when it is your turn. You, too, will think to yourself, "this is a good way to go." Because He died for you, Jimmy, so you won't have to hurt anymore.

The Lord once said to His friends that He was going to prepare a place for all of us (John 14:2). John saw the Revelation of Heaven, and wrote that "He will wipe every tear from their eyes. There will be no more death, or mourning or crying or pain, for the old order of things has passed away" (Rev 21:4).

Why are we so sad on Earth when our loved ones go home and come here? If we could take a moment, and just imagine the perfect Heaven for our family and friends when they leave Earth. What did they love to do? Who did they love to do it with? It is said, "What no eye has seen, what no ear has heard, and what no human mind has conceived—the things God has prepared for those who love him—these are the things God has revealed to us by his Spirit" (1 Cor. 2:9-10). Imagine your greatest Heaven, and God has something greater in store for you. The Lord has shown me how the Father had a place for me all along, both on Earth, and now in Heaven.

Then, I told Him that I loved Him, and I thanked Him for taking care of my son. I thanked Him for taking care of your brothers, your sister, and my wife… and I thanked Him for taking care of me.

Then, Christ told me I still had some unfinished business left to be completed.

He wanted me to share my story—with you. I asked Him how this was possible, since you are still on Earth, and I am now in Heaven.

He smiled and said, "Remember, Jim, that all things are possible with God."

So here is His message. And here is my story.

I love you, Jimmy, and I can't wait to see you again.

Love,

Dad

— *Epilogue* —

As my grandfather and I discussed my seventh grade homework assignment, I asked him everything that was needed to complete the worksheet. He answered the questions and smiled, and I remember him clicking his gum. He wore khakis, a yellow golf shirt and a thin rubber band around his wrist. He was a kind man, and I liked him.

"Grandpa," I asked. "What does it feel like to die? Is it scary?"

I was a pretty quiet kid and didn't like to put people on the spot... especially adults. But I knew about the times when he had suffered cardiac arrests. Everyone in the family was aware that he didn't have much of a functioning heart left, and something had happened to him in that ICU in 1982.

He told me about his experience in a very matter-of-fact way. He was good at describing things, and I remember the way he spoke.

Growing up, it seemed like everyone I knew had a grandfather who was in "The War." My cousins and I were aware our Grandpa had flown a plane in World War II, and there was even a small model P-47 Thunderbolt in my grandparents' dining room. Always, as I looked at that little plane underneath the glass bowl protecting it, I wanted to draw a tiny woodpecker next to the propeller to make it really look like Grandpa's plane.

Seventh grade meant that our class would be receiving the sacrament of Confirmation. I sat at my desk listening to our religion teacher recount the holy day of Pentecost:

"When the Day of Pentecost had fully come, they were all with one accord in one place. And suddenly there came a sound from heaven, as of a rushing mighty wind, and it filled the whole house where they were sitting. Then there appeared to them divided tongues, as of fire, and one sat upon each of them. And they were all filled with the Holy Spirit and began to speak with other tongues, as the Spirit gave them utterance." (Acts 2:1-4)

I knew what kinds of things my friends and I were thinking about and doing in the seventh grade, and I was fairly certain no tongues of fire would be appearing over our heads. Nevertheless, the Archbishop would be coming to our church for the Confirmation mass in just a few weeks.

We boys had been told that years before, the priest administering the sacrament would anoint one's forehead with holy oil, and then slap one's cheek, declaring that he or she was now a soldier for Christ. I was glad I wouldn't be getting slapped in the face, but I remember being intrigued by the idea of becoming a soldier of any kind.

Confirmation happened in our church at the age of twelve or thirteen because we were deemed old enough to make decisions of our own accord. The vow was for us to confirm our walk in Christ. But, before we were to get confirmed, we had to find another person to accompany us as our sponsor. Our teachers told us to choose someone other than a parent.

That was the first time I remember having an idea hit my brain and my heart at the same time. *"Grandpa."* I could feel the word in my mind and the weight of it in my chest. It wasn't exactly *heavy*, but more like *simultaneous*. Although I still gave the sponsor question some thought, my decision was made. I asked Grandpa to be my sponsor.

He told me that he would be honored, and I awkwardly told him that I was glad that he would be honored. Next, I had to invite him over to my house to talk about the Holy Spirit and then we had to write down our answers together. You know... normal stuff.

———

In April, 2015, I was given a moth-eaten stack of black papers after my grandmother had died a few years earlier. The paper fibers disintegrated in my hands; cloth tape held the old photos together in the stack. It was all that was left from a 1940s photo album.

I looked at the newspaper clippings and at the captions under the photographs: images from England, France and Germany, photos from the airbases on D-Day, flight logs from combat missions and tarnished medals rounding out the collection. Here were the stories of my grandfather's services in World War II and Korea, along with so many of his fellow patriots. It was astounding. Many in our family knew the stories, but I can't say I ever really *knew* the stories.

At first I was amazed, and then I was overwhelmed by the sheer amount of valuables. How would I preserve the leather jacket? Which of these medals should be displayed first? What did it really feel like to get shot at in the sky over an ocean?

Why hadn't I asked Grandpa these things before he died in 1993? Why hadn't I asked him anything important about his life?

And then that same Voice—the one I had heard back in seventh grade—hit my mind and my heart at the same time, again.

"You did ask him something."

———

I had asked him about the Light. I had asked him about the Voice and what God sounded like. This all came back to me in the spring of 2015, as I stared at the stack of old memorabilia. Accepting the challenge, I started piecing together Grandpa's story, and also working through the album with my family.

My grandfather's life influenced me when I was young; it continues to inspire me many years after his death. The Holy Spirit speaks to us through our hearts, through one another, and through the Word.

And that part, is my story.

— *Acknowledgements* —

There are many people who helped make this book possible, to whom I am grateful.

I want to thank my wife, Gina, for supporting me and listening to the story's many iterations. Of all my creative endeavors, this one has been an especially personal one. I love you, and I appreciate all your encouragement.

I am thankful for having been surrounded by such a loving family over the years, both immediate and extended. Jim "Grandpa Mac" McCabe, was with us on this Earth for seventy years. We are all so thankful for the blessing of both his amazing life, and the life of his loving wife, Mary, my grandmother.

I want to thank my father, Jim "Jimmy" McCabe, and my mother, Jane McCabe. Mom and Dad, I appreciate all you have done for me and my family.

I am thankful to my uncles, Denny and Mark McCabe, who were generous with their time in helping me piece together so many family facts and for answering all of my questions about life with their dad.

Thank you to my aunt, Peggy Kerckhoff, who provided me with a daughter's perspective of Grandpa, and for her insight and encouragement as I began this book. Thank you, also, to Meghan Baker for digging through the old albums and finding treasured photos.

I am grateful to the family of Nancy McCarthy, and to Nancy's children: Ann, Kathi and John. Thank you for taking the time to share more about your lives and the life of your late mother, Nancy McCabe McCarthy.

I would also like to acknowledge the help of my friend Fred O'Neill, who provided military and historical context for Jim's decorated service. Thank you to Sandy Aberle, for all of your editorial guidance and technical instruction in reviewing this work, to my friend Jeff Nourse, for generously donating professional expertise and advice. I would also like to thank Mike McCabe, LTC Brian McCall, CDR Tracy White, Sarah Wilson, and Brian Martindale.

Also assisting me in the research of this book was Dennis Northcott, Associate Archivist for Reference at the Missouri Historical Society, and Chris Naffziger and his online photography collection at St. Louis Patina.

To my friends Dan Deeble, Matt Gazaway, Ryan Hoover, and our whole Buoy group: thank you for all the spiritual encouragement you have shown me and my family over the years. And a big thanks to my cousin and author Kim Penny for your encouragement along the way.

There are many great resources available to further explore the subject of Heaven. My first recommendation would be to start with the Bible; the Gospel of John, the Book of Revelation, and the writings of St. Paul provided me with the most fascinating accounts of Heaven from the New Testament. Many accounts from the Old Testament predate the imagery of Heaven in the New Testament and are found in the accounts of Daniel, Ezekiel, and the Psalms.

I believe that God's will was always for Jim to return to Earth in 1982. Those "extra" twelve years of Jim's life were a blessing to all the family and friends who knew him, and we are forever thankful.

Lastly, to my children, Lia, Henry and Ollie: I pray that you will honor the legacy of the great men and women in your family tree. And I pray that someday, by the grace of God, we will all be reunited in His Kingdom to celebrate in eternity together, forever. Amen.

- Tim

— *Bibliography* —

"450 Horsepower Solo." *The United States Cartridge News* 15 Sep 1942: Print.

Bowlin, J B. "Letters Received by the Adjutant General, 1822-1860." *Fold3.com* 21 Dec 1846: Web. Accessed 29 May 2019.

"Brothers Fight In Same Raid Over Reich Without Knowing It." *St. Louis Star-Times* 31 Oct 1944: Print.

Chouteau, A R. "Letters Received by the Adjutant General, 1822-1860." *Fold3.com* 12 Dec 1846: Web. Accessed 29 May 2019.

"Club History." *St. Louis Hinder Club* 2017: thehinderclub.com/ SLHC_Home.html Web. Accessed 19 July 2018.

Cochran, Congressman John J. Letter to Mr. James McCabe, 8 June 1944. TS.

Field Press Offices, Ninth Air Force. Immediate Release - Public Correspondence to Mr & Mrs Harry D McCabe, Sr., 11 Oct 1944. TS.

Griffin, John J., Letter to Mr. and Mrs. Harry McCabe, Sr., 1 Nov 1944. TS.

Hallion, Richard P. "The Day After D-Day." *Air & Space Mag Online* May 2015: Web. Accessed 14 June 2019.

Harmon, Major General H.R. Letter to Mr. and Mrs. Harry D. McCabe, 29 Oct 1942. TS.

Hasserman. "D.F.C. Awarded Capt. J. McCabe." *St. Louis University Prep News* Oct 1944: Print.

"Helicopter Rescues St. Louis Pilot Shot Down Behind Enemy." *St. Louis Globe-Democrat* 28 Oct 1951: Print.

Irwin, Virginia. "Virginia Irwin Finds St. Louisans With 'Work Horse' P-47 Group." *St. Louis Post Dispatch* 25 Sept 1944: Print.

Knighton, Andrew. "How the US Navy Trained its Pilots in WWII - the Bar for Entry was High." *War History Online* 5 Oct 2017: Web. Accessed 28 May 2019.

Korean War Air Loss Database (KORWALD) Report Prepared 2015: Page Number 137, 2 Web. Accessed 22 Feb 2017.

McCabe, James J. Flight Log 3 June 1942 - 2 Sept 1943. *Collection of the Author.*

McCabe, James J. Flight Log 17 Nov 1943 - 17 Sept 1944. *Collection of the Author.*

McCabe, Captain James J. *XIX Tactical Air Command Combat Film* 11 April 1944 - 14 June 1944: youtube.com Web. *Collection of the Author.*

McEnnis, Michael. "Cholera, 1849." *Missouri History Museum Collection* circa 1907: Web. Accessed 2 June 2019.

McEnnis, Michael. "Coming to St. Louis, MO. from Baltimore, MD., in November, 1837." *Missouri History Museum Collection* circa 1910: Web. Accessed 6 June 2019.

McEnnis, Michael. "Letters Received by the Adjutant General, 1822-1860." *Fold3.com* 11 Dec 1846: Web. Accessed 29 May 2019.

"Michael McEnnis, Sole Survivor of 3600 of St. Louis' Bravest Youths." *St. Louis Post-Dispatch c/o Newspapers.com* 14 May 1911: Web. Accessed 29 May 2019.

Oliphint, USAF Captain John H., et al. "Evasion and Escape Report #63 Interrogation of F-51 Pilot Captain James J McCabe." *Headquarters Far East Air Forces APO 925 (Restricted)* 14 Nov 1951. TS.

Quesada, Brigadier General E.R. Letter to Mr. H. D. McCabe, 15 March 1944. TS.

Sides, Hampton. *Blood and Thunder: The Epic Story of Kit Carson and the Conquest of the American West.* New York: Anchor Books, 2006. Print.

Smith, Jeffrey. "Working the 'graveyard shift' at Ikea." *St. Louis Post-Dispatch Online* 12 June 2014: Web. Accessed 29 May 2019.

"St. Louis Pilot Tells Of Rescue In Korea." *St. Louis Post Dispatch* Aug 1952: Print.

"St. Louisans On Their Way to Wings." *St. Louis Star-Times* 24 Aug 1942: Print.

TLC. "Chris O'Donnell, Season 4, Episode 5." *Who Do You Think You Are?* 20 Aug 2013: TV. See: "Henry McCabe, Sarah McCabe, Regina McCabe, Michael McEnnis, George McNeir."

"War of 1812 Timeline." *American Battlefield Trust* https://www.battlefields.org/learn/articles/war-1812-timeline Web. Accessed 6 June 2019.

The events described in Chapters 1, 2, 4, 6, 8, 9, 10, 11, 12 and 13 are from Jim's life, and the lives of his relatives, and referenced in this Bibliography. The events described in Chapters 3, 5, 7, 9, 12 and 14 are based on Jim's experience in 1982, and the scriptural imagery of Heaven as described in both the New and Old Testaments.

All Scripture quotations, unless otherwise indicated, are taken from the Holy Bible, New International Version®, NIV®. Copyright ©1973, 1978, 1984, 2011 by Biblica, Inc.™ Used by permission of Zondervan. All rights reserved worldwide.

"The Star Spangled Banner," was written in 1814 by Francis Scott Key. The original poem, "Defence of Fort M'Henry," was used in this book in Chapter 10 in accordance with freedom of public domain. The accounts of George McNeir's service are based on records available at the Maryland State Archives and the Baltimore City Directories of 1812.

Michael McEnnis's account of his service and return to St. Louis in Chapter 11 is taken directly from his word-for-word typewritten accounts, "Cholera,

1849," and "Michael McEnnis, Sole Survivor of 3600 of St. Louis' Bravest Youths" courtesy of the public domain records available from the Missouri Historical Society and the St. Louis Post-Dispatch. The accounts are Michael's own, and they are attributed to him as his own words in this book.

Jim's account of his bailout and rescue in the Korean War in Chapter 4 is taken directly from his word-for-word typewritten account, "Evasion and Escape Report #63 Interrogation of F-51 Pilot Captain James J McCabe" dictated on November 14, 1951 by USAF Captain John H. Oliphant, et al.

Made in the USA
San Bernardino, CA
15 March 2020